The AI Engineer Roadmap

A Practical Guide to Python, PyTorch, Machine Learning, Cloud AI, Portfolio Projects, and Certification

PRACTICAL NOTEBOOK

Copyright and Publication

Published by Practical Notebook
Lille, France

ISBN: 9782489483994
Print on demand by Lightning Source / IngramSpark
Legal deposit: August 2026
First edition, 2026

This book provides educational and informational material, not personalized legal, financial, medical, employment, or certification advice. Verify current details with the relevant official source before acting. Certification names, company names, and trademarks belong to their respective owners. Practical Notebook is not affiliated with or endorsed by the organizations discussed unless explicitly stated.

Some optional publisher-controlled resource pages may contain affiliate links. Practical Notebook may earn a commission at no additional cost to the reader.

https://www.practicalnotebook.com

Contents

Introduction — From AI Interest to an Engineering Roadmap 5

Chapter 1 — What an AI Engineer Actually Does 10

Chapter 2 — Map Your Starting Point 18

Chapter 3 — Build Your Personal AI Engineer Roadmap 26

Chapter 4 — Python for AI Engineering 32

Chapter 5 — Machine Learning Without Drowning in Mathematics 42

Chapter 6 — Learn PyTorch by Building 51

Chapter 7 — Decide Where Certification Fits 61

Chapter 8 — The Certification Commitment 69

Chapter 9 — Project 1: From Data to Model 77

Chapter 10 — Project 2: Build a Modern AI Application 87

Chapter 11 — Project 3: Build With Production Constraints 98

Chapter 12 — Choose a Cloud Without Learning All Three 108

Chapter 13 — Linux, Containers, Kubernetes, and Your Production Milestone 116

Chapter 14 — Build Your Adaptable 12-Week Preparation Plan 124

Chapter 15 — Know When You Are Ready 134

Chapter 16 — Build a Portfolio That Explains Your Skills 141

Chapter 17 — Translate Skills Into a Resume 149

Chapter 18 — Prepare for AI Engineering Interviews 156

Chapter 19 — Your Next 12 Months 163

Conclusion — You Now Have a Path 170

Sources & Further Reading 172

Book Updates & Errata 175

Glossary 177

Appendix — Reusable Review Sheets 180

Appendix — Practice Lab Variants 188

Appendix — Interview Question Bank 192

INTRODUCTION

From AI Interest to an Engineering Roadmap

Interest in artificial intelligence is easy to acquire. A roadmap is harder.

You can open a browser and find a Python course, a machine learning specialization, a cloud certificate, a PyTorch tutorial, an agent framework, a collection of interview questions, and a promise that each one is the missing step. The problem is not a shortage of material. It is that the material arrives without a sequence.

That creates a familiar pattern. You study Python for a while, then hear that mathematics matters more. You move to linear algebra, then worry that you should be building projects. You start a project, but a job description mentions cloud deployment, Docker, and monitoring. A certification page offers a concrete syllabus, so you consider registering—then wonder whether the credential is respected, whether you are ready, or whether you chose the wrong cloud.

Activity increases while clarity decreases.

This book is designed to reverse that pattern.

> **Your goal is not to learn everything in AI. Your goal is to build the right sequence of skills.**

The sequence depends on the work you want to do, the evidence you already have, and the next constraint you need to remove. A software developer who can build reliable APIs but has never trained a model has a different starting point from a data analyst who understands evaluation but has never shipped a service. An infrastructure engineer may already understand Linux, containers, and monitoring while needing a stronger model-development foundation. Treating all three people as identical beginners wastes their experience and often sends them toward the wrong first milestone.

What this book will help you decide

The first part of the book separates several kinds of AI work that are often hidden behind similar titles. You will identify the work you actually want to perform, assess your current evidence, and choose one primary path:

- **Path A — AI / ML Engineer with PyTorch**
- **Path B — Cloud AI Application Engineer**
- **Path C — Production AI / MLOps Engineer**

The paths share a foundation, but they emphasize different work. Path A goes deeper into model development and PyTorch. Path B focuses on building dependable applications around model capabilities. Path C focuses on making AI systems repeatable, deployable, observable, and maintainable. You may eventually combine them. For the next learning cycle, however, you need a primary direction.

You will then establish enough Python, machine learning, and PyTorch understanding to make a meaningful certification decision. A certification can provide structure and a verifiable milestone. It cannot replace projects, practical judgment, or professional experience. The question is therefore not, "Which certificate will make me an AI engineer?" The useful question is, "Does a specific certification match the path I selected and the evidence I need to build next?"

Later parts of the book turn that decision into three connected projects. The first demonstrates that you can train and evaluate a model. The second demonstrates that you can build a modern AI application using existing model capabilities responsibly. The third demonstrates that you can reason about deployment, observability, reproducibility, cost, privacy, and reliability. Together, those projects create a more credible story than a disconnected collection of tutorial screenshots.

Finally, you will translate your work into a portfolio, resume evidence, interview preparation, and a twelve-month progression. The outcome is not a magical change in job title. It is a set of decisions and artifacts that make your next actions visible.

What this book does not promise

Reading a roadmap does not produce engineering skill. Doing the work does.

This book does not guarantee a job, a promotion, a salary, an exam result, or a fixed completion date. It does not teach every feature of Python, every machine learning algorithm, every cloud platform, or every part of production infrastructure. It is not a substitute for official documentation, hands-on practice, or feedback from experienced practitioners.

It is also not an exam guide. You will not find real certification questions, reconstructed questions, dumps, or confidential material here. When a certification appears, it is treated as one milestone within a broader engineering plan.

Why some information lives online

The most useful principles in this book should remain useful for years. Prices, exam policies, software versions, certification names, course catalogs, and cloud products can change much faster.

Practical Notebook resources separate those two kinds of information. The printed book explains the durable decision. A small number of contextual QR codes lead to publisher-controlled pages for current details, updated templates, and official links. You never need to scan a code to understand the method or complete the core exercises.

Some destination pages may contain affiliate links. When they do, that relationship is disclosed clearly. A commission does not change the decision gate in the book: a resource is relevant only if it solves the reader problem already identified. The book is not sponsored or endorsed by the organizations it discusses unless an explicit statement says otherwise.

Build evidence as you read

This is a working book. At the end of each part, you will have produced something:

1. a chosen role and primary path;
2. a skills-gap record;
3. a certification decision and commitment sheet;
4. three connected project artifacts;
5. a cloud and production architecture choice;
6. a personalized preparation plan;
7. a portfolio, resume, interview, and twelve-month action plan.

Write in the book. Mark uncertainty. Revise earlier decisions when new evidence justifies it. A crossed-out assumption followed by a better decision is progress, not failure.

Start with a fifteen-minute observation

Before reading Chapter 1, write one sentence. Do not name a course, framework, or certification. Describe something you want to be able to build, improve, or operate.

Examples:

- "I want to train and evaluate models for real product problems."
- "I want to build reliable applications that use modern model capabilities."
- "I want to make machine learning systems deployable and observable."

What I want to be able to do:

You do not need the perfect answer. You need a working hypothesis that Chapter 1 can test.

CHAPTER 1

What an AI Engineer Actually Does

Job titles compress complicated work into a few words. That makes them useful for search boxes and unreliable as roadmaps.

Two companies can advertise an "AI Engineer" role and expect very different days. One team needs a software engineer who can integrate a foundation-model API, build retrieval, validate structured responses, and operate the service. Another needs someone who can prepare training data, implement models in PyTorch, run experiments, and improve evaluation results. A third uses the title for a platform engineer who owns pipelines, containers, deployments, monitoring, and cost controls.

The title is not meaningless. It is simply incomplete.

Instead of asking which title sounds most exciting, examine five things:

1. What problem does the person own?
2. What artifact do they produce?
3. What decisions do they make?
4. What failure are they expected to diagnose?
5. What evidence would show that they can do the work?

Those questions create a more stable career map than a list of fashionable titles.

AI application engineering

An AI application engineer builds software that uses model capabilities to solve a user or business problem. The model may be trained by another team or provided through an API. The engineering work remains substantial.

Consider a system that answers questions from a controlled document collection. Calling a model is only one component. The application must ingest and segment documents, create or retrieve representations, select relevant context, construct requests, validate responses, handle permissions, measure answer quality, control latency and cost, protect sensitive data, and behave sensibly when evidence is missing.

The central question is not, "Can I make the model produce a response?" It is, "Can I build a reliable product behavior around a probabilistic component?"

Common evidence includes a working application, tests, an architecture diagram, an evaluation set, failure analysis, and documented tradeoffs. Strong application engineers usually need conventional software skills: APIs, data validation, authentication, error handling, logging, deployment, and maintenance.

Machine learning engineering

An ML engineer focuses more deeply on turning data and modeling methods into a system that can be evaluated and used. Depending on the organization, the work may include data preparation, feature or representation choices, model selection, training, experiment tracking, performance optimization, serving, monitoring, and retraining.

The artifact is not just a notebook containing a high score. It is a reproducible relationship among data, code, model state, evaluation, and operating constraints.

A useful ML engineer can explain why a metric matches the decision, where leakage may occur, how the baseline was chosen, what changed between experiments, and how the model will behave on new data. The role often sits between experimental work and software delivery. Some teams expect substantial production ownership; others hand trained artifacts to a platform group.

Path A in this book emphasizes this family of work and uses PyTorch as the primary framework for building model-development fluency.

Data science

Data scientists investigate questions with data. They may define metrics, design experiments, analyze behavior, build predictive models, estimate uncertainty, and communicate findings that influence a decision.

There is meaningful overlap with ML engineering, especially when data scientists train models. The distinction is often the center of gravity. A data scientist may be judged primarily on the quality of analysis and decision support. An ML engineer may be judged more heavily on repeatability, model behavior, integration, and operation.

Neither role is automatically more advanced. They optimize for different outputs. If you enjoy investigating ambiguous questions, testing explanations, and communicating evidence, data science may fit better than a roadmap centered on building and operating AI systems.

Production AI and MLOps engineering

Production-oriented AI engineers make model workflows dependable across environments and over time. They care about how code, data, model artifacts, configuration, infrastructure, and monitoring move from development to operation.

Their questions include:

- Can another person reproduce this result?
- Can the same artifact run in a controlled environment?
- What happens when input data changes?
- How will we detect degraded quality or increased latency?
- Which version of the data, code, and model produced this output?
- How do we roll back safely?
- What does this system cost under real traffic?

The work may involve Linux, containers, CI/CD, model registries, orchestration, observability, security, and cloud infrastructure. Kubernetes can become relevant, but it is not a universal entry requirement. A small, well-operated service is better evidence than a complex cluster copied from a tutorial.

Path C emphasizes this family of work.

Research roles

Research roles focus on creating, adapting, or rigorously testing methods at a deeper theoretical or experimental level. The work may involve novel architectures, optimization methods, training techniques, evaluation methodology, or scientific applications.

Research engineers often combine strong implementation skills with deeper mathematical and experimental work. Research scientists commonly require advanced academic preparation, although expectations vary by organization and problem.

If your primary desire is to invent new learning methods or publish original research, this book can help you organize engineering foundations, but it is not a research-training curriculum. You may need substantially more mathematics, research methods, and domain depth than the roadmap covers.

Compare the work, not the prestige

Use these role cards to compare the work itself. Each one names its center of gravity, the evidence it tends to produce, and a failure its practitioners may need to diagnose.

AI application engineer
Center: reliable software behavior using model capabilities.
Evidence: an application, tests, an evaluation set, and an architecture explanation.
Failure to diagnose: unreliable output, weak retrieval, or integration failure.

Machine learning engineer
Center: reproducible model development and delivery.
Evidence: a training pipeline, an evaluated model, and an experiment record.
Failure to diagnose: leakage, poor generalization, or training/serving mismatch.

Data scientist
Center: analysis, experiments, and decision evidence.
Evidence: an analysis, experiment or model accompanied by a decision memo.
Failure to diagnose: an invalid comparison, weak metric, or unsupported conclusion.

Production AI / MLOps engineer
Center: deployment, lifecycle, and operations.
Evidence: a pipeline, container, monitoring view, and runbook.
Failure to diagnose: drift, version mismatch, failed deployment, or cost spike.

Research engineer or scientist
Center: new or rigorously tested methods.
Evidence: experiments, implementations, or papers.
Failure to diagnose: a flawed method, irreproducible result, or invalid evaluation.

Real jobs can combine several cards. Use them to identify the work you want to own first, not to police titles.

Practical example: the same feature, five kinds of work

Imagine a company wants an internal assistant that answers questions from approved technical documents.

The application engineer designs the user flow, document-access checks, retrieval behavior, response validation, and service interface. The ML engineer may compare embedding or ranking approaches, build an evaluation set, measure retrieval quality, and optimize model behavior. The data scientist may analyze which questions employees ask and whether the system changes support outcomes. The production engineer builds deployment, monitoring, versioning, and incident procedures. A research team might investigate a new retrieval or adaptation method.

The product needs all of these perspectives. Your roadmap does not need to begin with all of them.

Transferable work is real evidence

Many readers arrive without an AI title. They may have automated a report, maintained a data pipeline, investigated a recurring incident, or built a small internal tool. Those experiences matter when you translate them into responsibilities and artifacts.

An analyst who defined a reliable metric already has evidence about measurement and ambiguity. A software developer who added tests and interfaces already understands parts of application engineering. An operations practitioner who wrote a runbook and restored a service already understands lifecycle and failure. The AI-specific gap still needs work, but the existing evidence can change the order and depth of the roadmap.

Do not erase transferable work because it is not branded as AI. Do not inflate it into model engineering either. Describe what you owned, what changed, and what remains different in the target path.

Role-fit worksheet

Complete these prompts with specific work rather than titles.

The problems I most want to own:

The artifacts I would enjoy building:

The failures I would be willing to investigate repeatedly:

The work I do not want as my primary focus:

Decision

Circle one working direction:

- building model-powered applications;
- training and evaluating models;
- investigating data and experiments;

- operating AI systems in production;
- pursuing deeper research.

This is a hypothesis, not a lifetime contract. Chapter 2 will test it against your current evidence. Chapter 3 will turn it into a primary learning path.

Next step

Do not search for another course yet. Open a blank page and list evidence you already possess for the direction you selected: code, analyses, deployments, documentation, experiments, or operational work. Chapter 2 begins with evidence, not confidence.

CHECKLIST

Chapter checklist

- [ ] I can explain why "AI Engineer" is not one standardized job.
- [ ] I selected work based on responsibilities, not title prestige.
- [ ] I can name an artifact that would demonstrate the work I want.
- [ ] I identified at least one kind of work I do not want as my primary focus.
- [ ] I have a working direction to test in the next chapter.

CHAPTER 2

Map Your Starting Point

A useful assessment does not ask whether you have "learned Python" or "know machine learning." Those phrases are too broad to guide a next step. It asks what you can do, explain, adapt, and debug.

Confidence is not reliable enough. Neither is course completion. A person may finish a long program by following instructions closely and still be unable to start a small project without the instructor's structure. Another person may underestimate years of transferable software or operations experience because it did not carry an AI title.

This assessment uses evidence. For each skill area, identify a task you can perform and how independently you can perform it.

The three working levels

Foundation means you cannot yet complete the core task without step-by-step instructions, or you can reproduce syntax without explaining the main choices.

Builder means you can complete a small task, explain the main choices, and make a limited change when the requirements shift.

Practitioner means you can adapt the skill to an unfamiliar but bounded problem, diagnose common failures, compare tradeoffs, and document the result for another person.

These labels are not credentials and are not a scientific score. They are planning categories. You may be a Practitioner in software delivery, a Builder in Python, and Foundation in model evaluation. That uneven profile is useful information.

Python

The relevant question is not whether you remember every language feature. It is whether Python can serve as a working engineering tool.

Foundation test: Read a short script that loads data, calls two functions, and prints a result. Identify the inputs, outputs, and control flow. Make one small change without copying a complete solution.

Builder test: Write functions that transform a small dataset, handle a foreseeable error, and separate reusable logic from an exploratory notebook. Create an isolated environment and record the required packages.

Practitioner test: Open an unfamiliar small project, trace a failure from the error message, add or modify behavior, write a focused test, and explain the dependency and interface choices.

Do not rate yourself on your best day with a familiar tutorial. Use a recent example you could show another engineer.

Git and collaborative change

Git is not merely a place to upload finished files. It records how a project changes.

Foundation test: Initialize or clone a repository, inspect its status, make a commit, and recover a file from an accidental local change.

Builder test: Work on a branch, write a useful commit message, compare changes, resolve a simple conflict, and use a `.gitignore` appropriately.

Practitioner test: Organize changes for review, keep commits understandable, investigate history, and collaborate without mixing unrelated changes.

A polished GitHub profile is not required at this stage. A traceable working process is.

Confidence is not a measurement

Confidence can be useful as a signal to investigate, but it is not evidence by itself. A reader who feels comfortable after a tutorial may still be unable to start from an empty repository. A reader who feels uncertain may have strong debugging and delivery habits that transfer immediately.

When confidence and evidence disagree, keep the evidence and design a small test. The test should be difficult enough to reveal the gap but bounded enough to finish. This protects beginners from shame and experienced practitioners from false reassurance.

Statistics and measurement

AI engineering requires enough statistical judgment to avoid treating every number as truth.

Foundation test: Explain mean, median, spread, sample, and the difference between an observation and a population claim in plain language.

Builder test: Explain why one average can hide important groups, why a small sample creates uncertainty, and why correlation alone does not establish cause.

Practitioner test: Select and defend measurements for a concrete decision, identify likely sources of bias, and communicate uncertainty without hiding behind jargon.

You do not need to perform advanced derivations to begin. You do need to recognize when your evidence is weaker than your conclusion.

Linear algebra intuition

For the next stage, intuition about representation matters more than hand-calculating large matrices.

Foundation test: Explain a vector as an ordered collection of values and identify the shape of a small table or tensor.

Builder test: Reason about compatible shapes, describe a matrix transformation at a high level, and understand why model parameters and batches have dimensions that must align.

Practitioner test: Diagnose shape and broadcasting problems, reason about batches and feature dimensions, and connect vector operations to model computation.

If notation is uncomfortable but you can reason accurately with shapes and operations, record the discomfort as a gap—not as proof that you cannot progress.

Machine learning concepts

Foundation test: Distinguish features from targets and classification from regression. Explain why a baseline matters.

Builder test: Define separate training and evaluation data, choose a plausible metric for a problem, explain overfitting, and identify a simple leakage risk.

Practitioner test: Design an evaluation that reflects intended use, compare models to a meaningful baseline, perform error analysis, and explain limitations.

If your only evidence is a score from a guided notebook, rate the specific tasks you understand rather than the notebook as a whole.

APIs and application interfaces

Foundation test: Explain request, response, endpoint, input, output, and error at a practical level.

Builder test: Call an API from Python, validate the response, handle timeouts or invalid data, and keep credentials out of source code.

Practitioner test: Design a small interface, document its contract, implement retries only where safe, test failure cases, and reason about authentication, rate limits, and idempotency.

This category is especially important for Path B, but all paths benefit from understanding how components communicate.

Cloud

Foundation test: Explain the difference among local execution, a hosted service, object storage, and a managed database without relying on one provider's product names.

Builder test: Deploy a small service or job, configure access, inspect logs, and explain where cost is generated.

Practitioner test: Select a suitable service category, define permissions, automate deployment, monitor behavior, and reason about reliability and cost tradeoffs.

A cloud certification is not required to rate yourself. Evidence can be a small deployed system with a clear explanation.

Docker and containers

Foundation test: Explain the difference between an image and a running container.

Builder test: Write or modify a Dockerfile, build an image, run it with configuration, expose the required port, and inspect logs.

Practitioner test: Reduce unnecessary image complexity, manage secrets and configuration safely, diagnose networking or startup failures, and use containers in a repeatable build or deployment process.

Do not rate Kubernetes knowledge here. Containers are a smaller, earlier unit of competence.

Linux

Foundation test: Navigate directories, inspect files, use command help, and understand absolute versus relative paths.

Builder test: inspect processes, permissions, environment variables, ports, and logs; run a Python process and diagnose a common permission or path error.

Practitioner test: automate routine operations, reason about services and resource use, troubleshoot from logs and process state, and work safely on a remote system.

Your evidence inventory

Complete one skill card at a time. On each card, record your current level, one piece of evidence you can point to, and the next task that would change your rating. Do not average the levels into a single flattering number.

Python — Level: _ *Evidence:* _____ **Next task:** ____

Git — Level: _ *Evidence:* ____ **Next task:** ____

Statistics — Level: _ *Evidence:* ___ *Next task:* _________

Linear algebra intuition — Level: _ *Evidence:* _ *Next task:* _________

Machine learning concepts — Level: _ *Evidence:* _ **Next task:** ____

APIs — Level: _ *Evidence:* _____ Next task: ______

Cloud — Level: _ *Evidence:* ____ Next task: ______

Docker and containers — Level: _ *Evidence:* __ **Next task:** ____

Linux — Level: _ *Evidence:* ____ Next task: ______

OPTIONAL RESOURCE

Interactive AI Engineer Path Assessment

The printed assessment is complete. Scan to save an editable version and update it as your evidence changes.

Save or update your assessment

www.practicalnotebook.com/the-ai-engineer-roadmap/assessment

Read the pattern, not just the labels

Now look across the rows.

If Python, ML concepts, and PyTorch-related experience are all weak, your next step is a structured foundation—not a certification purchase. If software, APIs, and cloud are stronger than model training, Path B may let you build credible evidence sooner. If Linux, Docker, CI/CD, and operations are strong, Path C can use that experience while you build ML fundamentals. If model evaluation and PyTorch are already your strongest categories, Path A may be the most direct fit.

The purpose of assessment is not to delay action until every row says Practitioner. It is to choose an action that is difficult enough to create evidence and small enough to complete.

Next step

Underline three rows: your strongest evidence, your most important shared foundation gap, and the skill most specific to the work you chose in Chapter 1. Chapter 3 uses those three rows to select a primary path.

CHECKLIST

Chapter checklist

- ☐ Every rating points to an observable task or artifact.
- ☐ I did not count course completion as proof by itself.
- ☐ I identified my strongest transferable skill.
- ☐ I identified the gap most likely to block my chosen work.
- ☐ I wrote the next task that would change each weak rating.

CHAPTER 3

Build Your Personal AI Engineer Roadmap

A roadmap is not a list of everything worth learning. It is an ordered set of constraints.

You need a primary path because the field contains too many legitimate directions to pursue at once. Choosing Path A does not declare cloud irrelevant. Choosing Path B does not mean you will never train a model. Choosing Path C does not excuse weak understanding of model evaluation. The choice determines which evidence you will build first and which attractive topics you will deliberately postpone.

The shared engineering foundation

All three paths require enough Python to read and modify working code, enough Git to make changes traceable, enough API understanding to connect components, enough data literacy to inspect inputs and outputs, enough ML evaluation to recognize misleading results, and enough security awareness to avoid obvious harm.

They also share a professional habit: documenting decisions. A project becomes more credible when another person can see the problem, constraints, architecture, evaluation, limitations, and next change.

Your path begins after that shared baseline, not instead of it.

Path A — AI / ML Engineer with PyTorch

Choose Path A when the work you want centers on training, adapting, evaluating, or optimizing models and when PyTorch is a sensible framework for the projects you want to build.

The sequence is:

1. establish working Python, NumPy, Git, and ML evaluation;
2. understand tensors, data pipelines, modules, loss, gradients, and optimization;
3. complete a small end-to-end PyTorch workflow;
4. build a portfolio project with a baseline, held-out evaluation, error analysis, and reproducibility;

5. learn how the model artifact is served and monitored;
6. add cloud and production depth according to the role you target.

PTCA may become a useful first certification milestone on this path. It should not be selected simply because it has no barrier to browsing or because PyTorch appears in the title. You will evaluate fit in Chapter 7 after establishing the relevant concepts.

Strong early evidence for Path A is not a collection of architecture names. It is a complete, explained experiment: where the data came from, what the baseline was, how the split was designed, what the model learned, where it failed, and what you would test next.

Path A is a good fit when you enjoy asking why a model changed, how a representation affects error, and whether an evaluation result survives a different split. It is a weaker fit when you mainly want to integrate a working model and are frustrated by data and experiment details. That does not disqualify you from AI engineering; it points toward Path B or a hybrid role.

Path B — Cloud AI Application Engineer

Choose Path B when you want to build software products using model capabilities and when integration, user behavior, reliability, and delivery interest you more than training models from scratch.

The sequence is:

1. strengthen Python or another application language, APIs, Git, tests, and data validation;
2. understand ML and foundation-model behavior well enough to evaluate outputs and failure modes;
3. build an application around an inference API or hosted model;
4. add retrieval, structured outputs, or bounded tool use only when the problem requires them;
5. create an evaluation set and measure behavior beyond a few impressive examples;

6. deploy with authentication, logging, cost controls, privacy boundaries, and monitoring.

This path is not "the easy route" because it can avoid training. The engineering difficulty moves into system behavior. Probabilistic outputs, changing models, untrusted inputs, access control, latency, cost, and evaluation create real design work.

A framework-focused certification may not be the best first credential for this path. A current cloud or role-based milestone may eventually fit better, but the certification names and statuses must be checked when you are ready to choose.

Path B is a good fit when you enjoy turning ambiguous user needs into interfaces, tests, boundaries, and feedback loops. The model is one component of a product whose behavior you must make understandable. If you prefer controlled experiments over user and system integration, keep Path A visible rather than assuming that an application title settles the choice.

Path C — Production AI / MLOps Engineer

Choose Path C when your strongest interest is making AI workflows reliable, repeatable, deployable, observable, and governable.

The sequence is:

1. establish ML lifecycle understanding from data and training through serving and monitoring;
2. strengthen Linux, Python automation, Git, testing, and configuration management;
3. containerize a small model or AI service;
4. build a reproducible pipeline with versioned code, data references, configuration, and artifacts;
5. automate validation and deployment;
6. monitor quality, reliability, latency, resource use, and cost;

7. add orchestration only when system scale and team needs justify it.

This path should not become an excuse to treat models as mysterious files. Production engineers need enough ML understanding to recognize training-serving mismatches, inappropriate metrics, data changes, and quality regressions.

Kubernetes may appear later. It is not your first proof. A small service with a clear build, test, deploy, monitor, and rollback story is more valuable than an unexplained cluster diagram.

Path C is a good fit when a failure report makes you curious about state, dependencies, recovery, and ownership. It requires patience with operational detail and a willingness to make invisible work visible through automation and documentation. It is not a refuge from programming or ML; it changes the questions you ask about them.

Choose with a constraint test

Use your evidence matrix from Chapter 2.

Choose **Path A** if model development is the work you want and your next limiting constraint is PyTorch/ML practice.

Choose **Path B** if application delivery is the work you want and your next limiting constraint is building reliable behavior around model capabilities.

Choose **Path C** if production ownership is the work you want and your next limiting constraint is connecting ML lifecycle knowledge to deployment and operations.

If two paths appear equal, choose the one that lets you complete a credible artifact within the next twelve weeks using more of your existing strengths. Momentum from a completed artifact is more useful than a theoretically perfect path that remains abstract.

My chosen role and primary path

The work I am targeting:

My primary path for the next twelve weeks: A / B / C

The strongest evidence I already bring:

The main constraint this path will remove:

The artifact I will complete:

Topics I am deliberately placing on my "not now" list:

Date I will review this path: ______

Next step

Keep this decision visible through Part II. Python, ML, and PyTorch are not separate collecting hobbies; they are foundations used in different proportions by your chosen path. When you reach Chapter 7, your primary path will determine whether PTCA deserves serious consideration or a clear "not yet."

CHECKLIST

Chapter checklist

- [ ] I chose one primary path, not a combined fantasy stack.
- [ ] My choice reflects work I want to perform.
- [ ] The path uses at least one existing strength.
- [ ] I named the constraint I need to remove next.
- [ ] I selected an artifact that can be completed and explained.
- [ ] I created a "not now" list.

CHAPTER 4

Python for AI Engineering

You do not need to master the whole Python language before building useful AI systems. You do need enough control to read unfamiliar code, change it intentionally, isolate dependencies, inspect failures, and leave behind a project another person can run.

That distinction matters. Beginners often treat Python as a syllabus: syntax first, then every data structure, then object-oriented programming, then algorithms, and only later a project. The result can be months of preparation without an artifact. The opposite error is copying a notebook whose cells happen to run while understanding neither the inputs nor the state carried between them.

The useful middle is task-based. Learn a language feature when it removes a specific engineering constraint. A function matters because repeated logic needs a name and a contract. An exception matters because external data and services fail. A module matters because one notebook has become difficult to reason about. A test matters because a change should not silently break behavior you already trust.

The minimum working model

Every Python program in this roadmap can be understood as four movements:

1. receive input;
2. validate or transform it;
3. perform the central computation;
4. return, store, or communicate an output.

When you open unfamiliar code, find those movements before studying individual syntax. Ask where data enters, which assumptions are checked, which function owns the main decision, and what observable output proves the program worked.

Consider a script that loads records, removes incomplete rows, calculates a feature, passes the resulting array to a model, and writes predictions. Even if several libraries are unfamiliar, the data flow gives you a map. You can inspect shapes and types at each boundary. You can replace one step without rewriting the whole program. You can decide where an error should be handled rather than surrounding everything with a broad exception.

Use names that expose this flow. `load_records`, `validate_schema`, `build_features`, and `evaluate_predictions` communicate more than `process1` or `do_data`. Good naming is not decoration. It reduces the amount of hidden context required to change the project safely.

Data structures are decisions

A list preserves an ordered collection. A dictionary associates keys with values. A set represents unique membership. A tuple often communicates a fixed grouping. These are not trivia questions; they make certain mistakes harder or easier.

If a record has named fields, a dictionary is usually clearer than remembering that index two means `duration_seconds`. If you need to eliminate duplicate identifiers, a set expresses that intention directly. If order matters, do not choose a structure that discards it.

For each collection, be able to answer:

- What does one element represent?
- Can it be missing?
- Is order meaningful?
- Must values be unique?
- What type should a consumer receive?
- How large could the collection become?

AI projects add arrays and tensors because numerical work needs shapes, data types, and efficient operations. A two-dimensional array might represent rows of examples and columns of features. A three-dimensional tensor might add sequence position or image channels. Before applying an operation, write the expected shape in plain language. Many “model problems” are really unexamined data-shape problems.

Functions create testable boundaries

A useful function does one coherent job and makes its expectations visible. It should not quietly load a file, mutate global state, train a model, print five diagnostics, and return an unrelated number.

Prefer a boundary such as:

```
def normalize_duration(seconds: float, maximum: float) -> float:
    if maximum <= 0:
        raise ValueError("maximum must be positive")
    return min(max(seconds / maximum, 0.0), 1.0)
```

This small function has an input contract, a foreseeable invalid case, and an output range that can be tested. The exact calculation is less important than the habits it demonstrates.

Write a short docstring when the purpose, units, side effects, or return value would otherwise be ambiguous. Type hints can make interfaces easier to inspect, but they do not automatically validate values at runtime. Use them as communication and tooling support, not as proof that the data is correct.

Errors should preserve information

When a program fails, the traceback is evidence. Read from the final exception upward until you find the first frame in code you control. Record the input, expected behavior, actual behavior, and smallest reproducible case.

Avoid this pattern:

```
try:
    run_everything()
except Exception:
    pass
```

It hides the failure and lets later steps act on an unknown state. Catch only errors you can handle meaningfully. If a file is optional, a missing-file branch may be sensible. If a required dataset has the wrong schema, stop with an error that names the missing fields. If an external call fails transiently, preserve enough context to decide whether a retry is safe.

Logging is more useful than scattered prints once a program has multiple stages or runs without you watching. A useful log says what stage ran, which non-sensitive identifier was involved, and what happened. It must not expose API keys, private records, or raw personal data.

Testing strategy for small projects

Test the boundary where a wrong assumption would be expensive. A pure transformation can use a small input with a known output. A loader can be tested with a missing column and an invalid type. A command can be tested with a temporary directory and an expected report. A model pipeline can be tested with a tiny fixture that checks shapes and the inference contract rather than pretending a unit test proves model quality.

Keep tests fast enough to run after every meaningful change. A slow integration or model-quality test can run separately, but its command and expected interpretation belong in the README. When a test fails, decide whether the behavior changed intentionally or the code broke. Do not silence a failing test merely because the new output looks plausible.

Testing is also a communication tool. A future collaborator can learn what the project considers important by reading the assertions. The best early tests protect contracts that would otherwise remain in your head.

Environments and dependencies

“It works on my machine” usually means the project depends on state that was never recorded.

Create an isolated environment for each project. Install packages into that environment. Record direct dependencies and the Python version you used. Keep secrets outside source code. A new collaborator—or your future self—should be able to create the environment without guessing which global packages happened to be present.

Dependency files serve different needs. A short project may record direct packages in a requirements file. A packaged application may use a project configuration with declared dependencies. Exact environment snapshots can support reproducibility, but copying hundreds of transitive packages into every small repository can obscure which libraries the project actually chose. Document the method you used and why.

Never commit a virtual-environment directory, a private key, a cloud credential file, or a `.env` containing secrets. Add local-only files to `.gitignore`, but remember that ignoring a file does not remove a secret already committed. If a credential enters version history, treat it as exposed and rotate it.

Notebooks and scripts have different jobs

Notebooks are excellent for exploration: inspecting data, trying transformations, plotting errors, and writing observations beside results. Their weakness is hidden execution state. A cell may depend on another cell that ran twenty minutes ago in an order the document no longer shows.

Before calling a notebook reproducible:

- restart the runtime;
- run all cells from top to bottom;
- remove unused experiments that change state;
- make data paths configurable;
- record dependencies;
- fix or record random seeds where comparison requires them;
- explain the expected outputs.

Move stable logic into functions or modules. Keep the notebook as a narrative layer that imports those functions. This lets tests exercise the logic without pretending the notebook interface is a production service.

Scripts are better for repeatable commands. A training script can accept a configuration, load data, train, evaluate, and write artifacts to a named output directory. A separate inference script can load a saved artifact and apply the same preprocessing contract. Separation makes it harder to use one preprocessing path during training and another during prediction.

NumPy and vectorized thinking

NumPy arrays make shape and data type explicit. Learn to create arrays, inspect `shape` and `dtype`, select rows and columns, combine arrays, reduce across an axis, and understand broadcasting well enough to predict the output shape.

Vectorization is not a commandment to eliminate every loop. It is a way to express operations over collections using library primitives that are often clearer and faster. The first goal is correctness. A concise array expression that you cannot explain is not an improvement over a readable loop.

Before combining two arrays, write their shapes. Before converting data types, ask what information could be lost. Integer division, floating-point precision, missing values, and unexpected object types can quietly change results. Inspect a small example by hand before trusting an operation across a large dataset.

Git as an evidence trail

Version control is part of the artifact, not a final upload step. Initialize the repository before the project becomes complicated. Commit one understandable change at a time. A useful commit message names the behavior changed: "add validation for missing target values" is more informative than "updates."

Keep generated data, large model files, credentials, and environment directories out of ordinary Git history unless the project has an explicit storage strategy. Record how artifacts are obtained or regenerated. If a model file is too large to store, the README should still explain which command produces it and what metrics to expect within reasonable variation.

Branches are useful when a change needs isolation or review. They are not a requirement for every five-minute personal edit. The durable habit is to inspect the diff before committing and avoid mixing unrelated changes.

A small repository exercise

Build a command-line program that reads a small CSV file, validates required columns, calculates two summary features, and writes a cleaned CSV plus a text report.

Your repository should contain:

- a README explaining the input and output;
- a dependency declaration;
- a module with loading, validation, and transformation functions;
- a command or script that connects the functions;
- at least three focused tests;
- a sample input that contains no private data;
- a `.gitignore` appropriate to the project.

Test one valid case, one missing-column case, and one edge case such as an empty input or invalid numeric value. Run the program from a clean environment. Then change one requirement—for example, make a threshold configurable—and record the change in a separate commit.

The exercise is complete when another person can follow the README without asking which cell to run first.

Diagnose the real foundation gap

Rate the following with evidence:

- [ ] I can trace input through several functions to an output.
- [ ] I can write and call a function without copying a complete solution.
- [ ] I can create an isolated environment and record dependencies.
- [ ] I can read a traceback and reproduce a failure.
- [ ] I can inspect array shapes and reason about a simple transformation.
- [ ] I can move stable notebook logic into a module.
- [ ] I can write a focused test and explain what it protects.
- [ ] I can use Git to preserve understandable changes.

If one or two items are weak, repair them with targeted practice. If Python, machine-learning concepts, and the ability to trace a PyTorch workflow are all weak, a coherent structured foundation may be more efficient than assembling disconnected tutorials.

Next step

Keep the repository. Chapter 5 will add a prediction problem, a baseline, and an evaluation contract. The goal is not to replace the program with a mysterious model. It is to add machine learning while preserving the engineering discipline you just practiced.

CHECKLIST

Chapter checklist

- [ ] I completed the small repository from a clean environment.
- [ ] My README identifies inputs, outputs, setup, and commands.
- [ ] My code separates loading, validation, transformation, and reporting.
- [ ] I tested a normal case and at least two failure or edge cases.
- [ ] No secret or private dataset appears in version history.
- [ ] I selected targeted repair or a structured foundation for a written reason.

CHAPTER 5

Machine Learning Without Drowning in Mathematics

Machine learning is not the act of choosing an impressive algorithm. It is the discipline of using data to build a system whose behavior on unseen cases is useful enough for a defined decision.

That definition places the difficult questions in the right order. What is the prediction supposed to support? What counts as an example? Which information would exist at the moment of prediction? What baseline must the model beat? Which mistakes matter most? How will you detect when the result is weaker than it looks?

Mathematics helps answer these questions precisely, but you do not need to finish an advanced mathematics curriculum before you can reason responsibly about a first supervised-learning project. You need enough intuition to recognize shapes, uncertainty, optimization, and evaluation errors—and enough humility to stop when the decision requires expertise you do not yet have.

Start with the decision

A model maps inputs to an output. A product or organization then uses that output to make or support a decision. If the decision is vague, a good metric can still optimize the wrong thing.

Suppose a support team wants to predict whether a ticket needs specialist review. The target is not "important ticket" unless importance has an operational definition. The prediction time matters: features created after a specialist has already intervened cannot be used at intake. The cost of missing a ticket may differ from the cost of reviewing an extra one.

Write five statements before opening a modeling library:

1. **Decision:** what action may change because of the prediction?
2. **Unit:** what does one row or example represent?
3. **Target:** what observable outcome are you trying to predict?
4. **Prediction moment:** what information exists when the model must act?
5. **Harmful error:** which mistake deserves special attention?

This framing becomes part of the model contract. It also helps you recognize when a model is unnecessary. A deterministic rule may be cheaper, clearer, and more reliable for a stable threshold or policy.

Features, targets, and examples

Features are inputs available to the model. The target is the value the model is trained to predict. In supervised learning, examples connect features with known targets.

Classification predicts a category, such as whether a ticket should be escalated. Regression predicts a numeric value, such as expected resolution time. Real systems may use ranking, forecasting, anomaly detection, generation, or other formulations, but classification and regression teach the central habits clearly.

The row is not always the independent unit you think it is. Ten records from one customer, patient, device, or time period may share information. If related records appear in both training and test sets, evaluation can become unrealistically easy. Group or time-aware splitting may be necessary.

Ask whether the target itself is trustworthy. Historical decisions can reflect inconsistent processes or bias. A label produced by a previous model may encode that model's mistakes. Missing labels may not be random. Document who or what created the target and which disagreements it hides.

Build a baseline first

A baseline is a simple reference that the model must improve upon. For imbalanced classification, always predicting the majority class can achieve high accuracy while failing the useful cases. A better baseline may be a simple rule, a constant prediction evaluated with the right metric, or a straightforward linear model.

The baseline does three jobs. It exposes whether the problem contains a learnable signal. It catches pipeline mistakes when a sophisticated model performs suspiciously poorly—or impossibly well. It defines what "improvement" means.

Do not change the baseline after seeing the final test result merely to make the project look stronger. Record it before the main comparison.

Train, validation, and test roles

Training data is used to fit model parameters. Validation data supports choices such as model family, features, thresholds, and hyperparameters. Test data is reserved for a final estimate after those choices.

If you repeatedly inspect test performance and change the model in response, the test set has become part of development. Its estimate is no longer an untouched view of unseen behavior. For small datasets, cross-validation can use multiple train/validation partitions to estimate variability, but it does not remove the need to define what remains genuinely held out.

Split before learning preprocessing parameters. If a scaler, imputer, feature selector, or vocabulary is fitted using the whole dataset, information from evaluation rows influences training. This is data leakage even when the target column was never deliberately copied.

Time-dependent problems require special care. Training on future behavior to predict the past can produce an attractive but impossible result. Preserve the direction of time and simulate the information available at the real prediction moment.

Overfitting and generalization

A model overfits when it learns patterns that perform well on training data but do not generalize to relevant unseen data. More parameters, more features, repeated tuning, leakage, and small or unrepresentative samples can all contribute.

The remedy is not automatically a simpler algorithm. You may need better data, a more realistic split, regularization, a stronger baseline, fewer leaked features, a different metric, or a narrower claim.

Generalization is always relative to a population and operating context. A model evaluated on last year's customers may not generalize to a new region or changed product. A random split may not represent a future deployment. State where the evaluation data came from and where you expect the model to be used.

Loss and optimization

During training, a loss function converts prediction error into a number the optimization process can reduce. The optimizer updates parameters using gradients—directions that indicate how small parameter changes affect the loss.

You do not need to derive every gradient to understand the loop:

1. the model receives a batch of inputs;
2. it produces outputs;
3. the loss compares outputs with targets;
4. automatic differentiation computes gradients;
5. the optimizer updates parameters;
6. the process repeats over batches.

Loss is not automatically the business or user metric. A classification model may train with a loss suited to probability estimation while the project is evaluated using precision, recall, calibration, latency, and the consequences of false decisions.

Optimization can fail visibly or quietly. A learning rate may be too high, causing unstable loss, or too low, causing negligible progress. Incorrect shapes may trigger an error; incorrectly encoded targets may produce training that runs but means something else. Record curves and inspect examples rather than treating a completed loop as evidence of learning.

Choose metrics from mistakes

Accuracy measures the proportion of correct predictions. It can be appropriate when classes and error costs are reasonably balanced. It is inadequate when one class dominates or one error matters much more.

Precision asks: among items predicted positive, how many were positive? It matters when false positives are costly.

Recall asks: among actual positives, how many did the model find? It matters when missed positives are costly.

The balance between them depends on the decision threshold and use case. An F-score combines precision and recall, but the combined number can hide which kind of error changed. Report the components.

For regression, mean absolute error expresses average absolute deviation in target units. Squared-error measures penalize larger errors more strongly. A single average can hide systematic failure for important groups or ranges.

Metrics do not decide ethics or acceptable risk. In consequential domains, subgroup analysis, calibration, human review, privacy, and domain-specific validation may be essential. This roadmap does not authorize deployment in a high-stakes setting.

Calibration and decision thresholds

A score can be useful for ranking without being a reliable probability. If a system says “0.8,” ask what that number means in the evaluation context and whether users interpret it correctly. Calibration checks whether predicted probabilities correspond reasonably to observed frequencies; it does not make a model fair, safe, or correct.

Threshold selection is a policy choice. Lowering a threshold may increase recall while creating more reviews. Raising it may reduce workload while missing more positives. Show the tradeoff and identify who has authority to choose it. Do not hide a threshold inside a model file where the operator cannot inspect or change it deliberately.

When the output is used for ranking, report ranking behavior and the number of items surfaced. When it is used for a binary action, report the confusion matrix and error costs. The metric follows the decision.

Error analysis turns a score into engineering work

After calculating metrics, inspect failures. Group them by meaningful conditions: missing fields, rare categories, short text, long text, low-confidence predictions, time period, data source, or other non-sensitive operational factors.

For each cluster, ask:

- Is the label reliable?
- Was required information missing?
- Is the feature representation inadequate?
- Does the split expose a distribution difference?
- Would a threshold change help, and whom would it hurt?
- Is the model being asked to infer something the input cannot contain?

Do not browse private records casually. Use access controls, minimize copied data, and redact examples in public documentation. A portfolio should show the reasoning without exposing the people represented by the data.

The minimum mathematics ladder

Learn mathematics in response to the decisions you need to make.

Functions: understand an output as depending on inputs. This supports model composition and loss reasoning.

Vectors and matrices: understand shapes, rows, columns, dot products at an intuitive level, and transformations between representations.

Probability: understand uncertainty, conditional thinking, expected behavior, and why a predicted score is not automatically a trustworthy probability.

Distributions and samples: understand that observed data is a sample shaped by collection choices and that averages can hide variation.

Derivatives and gradients: understand local rate of change and why optimization follows a direction that reduces loss.

When a project exposes a gap, study the smallest mathematical unit that lets you explain the behavior, then return to the project. Do not use "more math" as an indefinite reason never to build.

Model experiment card

Complete this before training:

Decision supported: ________

One example represents: ________

Target and how it was created: ________

Information available at prediction time: ______

Baseline: ____________

Split strategy and leakage risk: ________

Primary metric and why it fits: ________

Most harmful error: ________

Groups or conditions requiring separate review: ______

Rule for deciding whether the experiment is useful: __

Run a disciplined first experiment

Use a small, non-sensitive dataset. Begin with a baseline and one simple model. Preserve the split. Fit preprocessing on the training portion only. Record the configuration, result, and one error-analysis observation.

Then change one meaningful variable: a feature representation, model capacity, regularization choice, threshold, or data-quality rule. State the hypothesis before running it. Compare against the baseline and previous experiment. Do not run twenty variations and report only the winner.

The result may be that the model does not beat the baseline reliably. That is still useful evidence if the experiment is reproducible and the limitations are explained honestly.

Next step

Bring the experiment card into Chapter 6. PyTorch will add tensors, modules, gradients, and an explicit training loop. The quality of the project will still depend on the framing and evaluation decisions made here.

CHECKLIST

Chapter checklist

- [ ] I framed a decision, unit, target, prediction moment, and harmful error.
- [ ] I selected a baseline before the main model.
- [ ] My evaluation rows did not influence learned preprocessing.
- [ ] My split reflects groups or time when necessary.
- [ ] I chose metrics by their relationship to mistakes.
- [ ] I inspected failures instead of reporting only one score.
- [ ] I recorded limitations and a next experiment.

CHAPTER 6

Learn PyTorch by Building

PyTorch makes the mechanics of model training visible. That visibility is valuable only if you connect each object to the experiment contract from Chapter 5.

This chapter builds a small binary classifier. The lab is intentionally bounded: it proves that you can trace data through a PyTorch workflow, modify the workflow, diagnose common failures, evaluate held-out behavior, and save an artifact. It is not a portfolio centerpiece and it is not certification preparation.

Use a small, non-sensitive tabular dataset with numeric features and a binary target. You may reuse the Chapter 5 experiment if the data fits. Keep the dataset small enough to train on a CPU. The goal is to understand the system, not to win a benchmark.

Establish the repository contract

Create a new branch or repository with this structure:

```
pyproject-or-requirements file
README.md
data/README.md
src/
  data.py
  model.py
  train.py
  evaluate.py
tests/
artifacts/
```

The data README should describe the source, license or permission, unit of analysis, target, exclusions, and whether the raw data may be redistributed. If raw data should not enter the repository, document how an authorized reader obtains it and provide a tiny synthetic fixture for tests.

The top-level README should identify the decision, baseline, split, metric, setup command, training command, evaluation command, output artifacts, and known limitations.

Tensors: values with shape and type

A tensor stores values and metadata such as shape, data type, and device. Print all three at key boundaries during early development.

If X contains 500 examples and 12 features, its expected shape is `[500, 12]`. A binary target might have shape `[500]` or `[500, 1]` depending on the loss and model output contract. Neither shape is universally correct; consistency is.

Convert numeric features to a floating-point type appropriate for the model. Encode targets according to the chosen loss. Do not "fix" a mismatch by repeatedly adding or removing dimensions until the error disappears. Write the intended shapes, read the loss documentation, and make the contract explicit.

Create a test that loads a small fixture and asserts feature count, target shape, absence of unexpected missing values, and data types. This catches upstream changes before training produces confusing behavior.

Dataset and DataLoader

A `Dataset` defines how many examples exist and how one example is retrieved. A `DataLoader` groups examples into batches and can shuffle training order.

Keep splitting separate from batch construction. First create train, validation, and test indices according to the experiment design. Fit preprocessing only on training data. Then create datasets and loaders for each partition.

Shuffle the training loader when example order has no intended sequential meaning. Do not shuffle evaluation merely from habit. Use a batch size that fits the available hardware and does not obscure the code. Larger batches are not automatically better.

Inspect one batch before defining the full training loop:

```
features, targets = next(iter(train_loader))
print(features.shape, features.dtype)
print(targets.shape, targets.dtype)
```

Confirm that the batch represents what you think it represents. A pipeline that cannot explain one batch is not ready to train thousands.

Define the model boundary

A PyTorch model commonly subclasses `nn.Module`. Its constructor defines layers; its `forward` method defines how input moves through them.

For the lab, use a small multilayer network or a single linear layer appropriate to the data. More layers do not make the exercise more authentic. A simple model makes shape and optimization errors easier to see.

The model should receive a batch shaped `[batch_size, feature_count]` and return one score per example. Keep probabilities, class decisions, and raw model outputs distinct. Many classification losses expect raw logits and apply the numerically stable transformation internally. Applying a sigmoid twice changes the training behavior.

Write a forward-pass test. Given a fixture batch, assert the output shape and that the values are finite. This is not a quality test; it protects the interface.

Loss, gradients, and the optimizer step

The training loop has a strict order:

1. move the batch to the selected device;
2. clear gradients from the previous step;
3. run the forward pass;
4. calculate loss;
5. run backpropagation;
6. update parameters;

7. record the batch loss.

Gradients accumulate by default. Forgetting to clear them changes the update. Updating parameters before backpropagation is meaningless. Calculating validation behavior while the model remains in the wrong mode can make results inconsistent for layers whose behavior changes between training and evaluation.

Use `model.train()` during training. Use `model.eval()` for validation and test evaluation, and disable gradient tracking when gradients are unnecessary. These calls communicate intent and prevent avoidable work or mode-dependent surprises.

Record average loss per epoch, not only the final batch. Also calculate the Chapter 5 evaluation metrics on validation data. Training loss alone cannot show whether the model generalizes or whether the selected threshold supports the decision.

Device handling without mythology

The device may be a CPU or an available accelerator. Choose it once and move both the model and every relevant tensor consistently. A common failure occurs when model parameters live on one device and inputs live on another.

Do not make accelerator access a prerequisite for this lab. A small model that runs predictably on a CPU teaches the same control flow. Performance engineering becomes useful when the workload creates a measured constraint.

Record the environment and device in the run output. Reproducibility includes knowing where the result came from.

Repeatability and randomness

Random seeds can make comparison easier, but they do not guarantee identical results across every hardware, library version, or operation. Record seeds, software versions, split identifiers, and configuration. Report reasonable variation rather than promising bit-for-bit reproduction everywhere.

Preserve the data split separately from the model. If every experiment creates a new random split, you may compare different evaluation samples rather than different modeling decisions.

Write run artifacts into a new directory containing:

- configuration;
- split or split identifier;
- training and validation history;
- final metrics;
- model state;
- environment information;
- notes about the hypothesis and result.

Do not overwrite the previous run automatically. Comparison requires history.

Evaluation and threshold choice

Evaluate on validation data during development. Compare against the baseline. Inspect precision, recall, or other metrics relevant to the error costs. If you choose a probability threshold, choose it using validation behavior and document the tradeoff.

Use the test set only after the pipeline and decision rule are settled. Report the result as an estimate for the defined test context, not as permanent model quality.

Inspect examples around the threshold and examples from the largest error clusters. Check whether incorrect labels, missing information, or group differences explain failures. A neural network does not remove the data questions from Chapter 5.

Save the right artifact

Saving model parameters is not enough if inference also depends on feature order, scaling, category encoding, threshold, or label mapping. Save or document the entire inference contract.

At minimum preserve:

- the model architecture or the code version that defines it;
- the model state;
- preprocessing parameters fitted on training data;
- ordered feature names;
- decision threshold;
- label meaning;
- library and Python versions;
- the evaluation record.

Load the saved artifact in a fresh process and run one known example. This "round-trip" test catches projects that can train but cannot be reused.

Read a run like a reviewer

Open one completed run without looking at the training code first. Can you identify the data version, split, model configuration, threshold, metric, device, and limitations from the saved record? If not, the project has produced an output but not an explainable artifact.

Compare two runs that differ in one declared variable. Explain whether the change moved the metric, the error groups, the latency, or the reproducibility. If you cannot tell what changed, improve the run record before adding another experiment. A reader who can reconstruct the reasoning has more evidence than a reader who can show a single high score.

Diagnose common failures

Shape error: write expected shapes at the model input, output, and loss boundary. Inspect one batch rather than guessing.

Loss does not decrease: verify targets, output/loss compatibility, learning rate, preprocessing, gradients, and whether parameters are included in the optimizer.

Training improves while validation degrades: investigate overfitting, leakage, split quality, model capacity, regularization, and data representativeness.

Metrics look impossibly strong: check duplicate or related records across splits, post-outcome features, target-derived features, and preprocessing fitted before splitting.

Loaded model changes behavior: verify evaluation mode, preprocessing, feature order, threshold, code version, and saved state.

Training is slow: measure data loading and computation before adding complexity. Confirm that the lab's model and dataset are appropriately small.

The modification test

A copied training loop becomes yours only when you can change it intentionally.

Make three modifications:

1. add or remove one hidden layer and predict how parameter count and overfitting risk may change;
2. change one optimization setting and state the hypothesis before training;

3. add a data-quality failure to the fixture and make the loader reject it clearly.

For each change, record expected behavior, observed behavior, and what you learned. Revert changes that do not improve the decision or the clarity of the project.

Annotated training-loop artifact

Draw the loop and label:

batch input → model output → loss → gradients → parameter update

Add side arrows for training mode, validation mode, device movement, metrics, and saved artifacts. Beside each arrow, write one failure that would occur if the step were wrong.

Then point to the corresponding function in your repository. The diagram should explain the code; the code should make the diagram true.

Path check before Chapter 7

You are ready to evaluate the Path A certification gate if you can:

- [ ] explain the shape and type of one batch;
- [ ] trace data through the model to the loss;
- [ ] explain why gradients are cleared and when parameters update;
- [ ] distinguish training, validation, and test use;
- [ ] run evaluation in the correct mode without tracking gradients;
- [ ] compare the model against a baseline using a relevant metric;
- [ ] save and reload the inference contract;
- [ ] modify the workflow and diagnose at least one failure.

If several items remain unsupported, Chapter 7 should produce "not yet." Return to the smallest missing piece. Do not memorize certification language around a workflow you cannot operate.

Next step

Preserve the repository and experiment record. Chapter 7 will not test whether you memorized an exam. It will ask whether a certification milestone follows your selected work and whether this practical evidence is strong enough to make the decision responsibly.

CHECKLIST

Chapter checklist

- [ ] My repository runs from a documented clean setup.
- [ ] Data, model, training, and evaluation responsibilities are separated.
- [ ] My split and preprocessing avoid known leakage.
- [ ] I inspected one batch and tested the model interface.
- [ ] I recorded configuration, metrics, and limitations.
- [ ] I loaded the saved artifact in a fresh process.
- [ ] I completed the modification test without copying a full replacement.
- [ ] I can explain why this lab is evidence of foundation, not professional experience.

CHAPTER 7

Decide Where Certification Fits

A certification is useful only when it supports work you have chosen. It can define a study boundary and record that you passed an assessment under a provider's current rules. It cannot choose your role, replace project evidence, or prove that you can design and operate an entire AI system.

This chapter therefore begins with the path, not the product. Path A readers can make an actionable PyTorch certification decision now. Path B readers should wait until they have built application evidence and chosen a cloud ecosystem. Path C readers should wait until Linux, containers, deployment, and operational work give a cloud-native milestone real meaning.

A correct outcome may be "yes," "later," or "not needed."

What a certification can signal

A well-matched credential can reduce a specific uncertainty. It may show familiarity with a published framework scope, a cloud role, foundational concepts, or a production technology. It can also turn an unbounded subject into a finite preparation plan.

The signal is narrower than professional competence. A credential does not by itself demonstrate that you can:

- frame a useful problem;
- choose and defend an evaluation method;
- build maintainable software;
- diagnose unfamiliar failures;
- communicate tradeoffs;
- operate a system responsibly;
- collaborate with other people.

Nor does it guarantee an interview, job, salary, promotion, or exam result. Your portfolio must carry the evidence the credential cannot.

Before selecting anything, finish this sentence:

> This credential would reduce uncertainty about____, **while my projects must still demonstrate______**.

If you cannot name the uncertainty, you do not yet have a reason to buy.

Four credential families

Framework-focused credentials cover a defined technology such as PyTorch. They can suit a reader who has already chosen model development and has enough foundation to understand the framework in context.

Cloud role credentials organize knowledge around one provider and a role. They can suit a Path B reader after the ecosystem choice is grounded in target work and application evidence. Because catalogs change, the current name and status belong on an updateable online page.

Foundational credentials establish broad concepts. They may provide an early milestone, but they are not evidence of advanced application engineering or production ownership.

Production and cloud-native credentials cover Linux, containers, Kubernetes, administration, development, or platform engineering. They can suit Path C at different maturity levels. They should follow hands-on evidence, not precede it.

No family is universally superior. The useful sequence is role → path → evidence gap → milestone.

Timing by path

Path A — AI / ML Engineer with PyTorch

Evaluate a framework-focused milestone now if you can already use basic Python, explain core machine-learning concepts, and trace a small PyTorch workflow. A current PyTorch credential may give this phase a clear boundary, but the next projects must still demonstrate training, evaluation, reproducibility, and engineering judgment.

Path B — Cloud AI Application Engineer

Do not select a cloud credential merely because its title contains "AI." First build evidence with APIs, retrieval or other model-enabled application behavior, evaluation, security, latency, and cost. Then choose one cloud ecosystem in Chapter 12 based on target roles and practical constraints. That is your cloud credential decision point.

Path C — Production AI / MLOps Engineer

Do not choose Kubernetes or platform credentials for prestige. First build Linux and container evidence, operate a small service, and understand deployment, reproducibility, observability, and the model lifecycle. Chapter 13 is your production milestone decision point.

Foundation not ready

If Python and machine-learning concepts are still the main blockers, the next milestone is structured learning and a small project—not an exam registration. Official free resources remain a valid route.

Where PTCA fits for Path A

The PyTorch Certified Associate, or PTCA, is currently positioned as a PyTorch-focused certification. It may be an appropriate first bounded milestone for a Path A reader who already has basic Python and machine-learning knowledge and has begun working through a real PyTorch workflow.

"First bounded milestone" is the important phrase. PTCA is not a complete AI engineer qualification. It does not replace evidence of problem framing, data decisions, baselines, evaluation, reproducibility, documentation, serving, or production awareness.

Prices, exam delivery, eligibility windows, retake rules, refunds, and even certification catalogs can change. The book deliberately does not freeze those details. Verify them from the current Practical Notebook page and the official provider before any financial decision.

The PTCA decision gate

Complete this gate only if Path A is your current path.

CHECKLIST

PTCA may fit now if

- [ ] Path A—AI / ML Engineer with PyTorch—is my selected direction.
- [ ] I can use basic Python without copying every step.
- [ ] I can explain supervised learning, evaluation, overfitting, and leakage in practical terms.
- [ ] I have traced and modified a small PyTorch workflow using data, a model, loss, gradients, and optimization.
- [ ] I want a bounded PyTorch milestone rather than a substitute for projects.
- [ ] I accept that the credential cannot guarantee employment or replace portfolio evidence.

CHECKLIST

Wait if

- [ ] I am still choosing among Paths A, B, and C.
- [ ] I cannot yet trace a basic training workflow.
- [ ] Weak Python or ML foundations would turn preparation into memorization.
- [ ] I lack realistic preparation capacity.
- [ ] I have not reviewed the current provider policies.
- [ ] Paying would crowd out the hands-on work I need more.

CHECKLIST

Choose a later path-specific gate if

- ☐ My main goal is building cloud AI applications with existing model capabilities.
- ☐ My main goal is production AI, infrastructure, platform engineering, or MLOps.
- ☐ My target roles consistently require a different kind of current evidence.

Make the decision explicit

Choose one decision before reviewing the current certification details.

Decision A — PTCA is my current target.

I selected it because:

The project evidence I must still build is:

Decision B — PTCA is not my next step yet.

Before reconsidering it, I will complete:

My review date is: ______

Decision C — Another credential family better fits my path.

My path is: ______

My later decision point is:

- [ ] Chapter 12 — cloud ecosystem and cloud credential
- [ ] Chapter 13 — production or cloud-native milestone
- [ ] No certification currently needed

If you selected Decision B or C, continue to Chapter 8 without scanning. The book remains complete, and your later gate will use the same decision framework.

Decision A only — check current PTCA fit and details

Next step

Chapter 8 separates certification selection, registration, and scheduling. Path A readers can use it immediately. Path B and C readers can record a target credential type, a “not selected yet” status, and the later chapter where the decision will be made.

CHECKLIST

Chapter checklist

- ☐ I can name the uncertainty a credential would reduce.
- ☐ I separated credential scope from job competence.
- ☐ My timing follows my chosen path.
- ☐ I made Decision A, B, or C before encountering the Path A QR.
- ☐ I named the project evidence that remains necessary.
- ☐ I know where my next path-specific decision occurs.

OPTIONAL RESOURCE

Current PTCA Fit & Details

Use this page only if Decision A is your current conclusion. Review the current scope, official policies, fit criteria, and registration options. If you are not ready, save the page and return when the decision becomes relevant.

Check current PTCA fit and details

www.practicalnotebook.com/the-ai-engineer-roadmap/certification/path-a

CHAPTER 8

The Certification Commitment

A certification plan becomes useful when its decisions are observable. “Someday” is not a decision; neither is paying before you understand the target.

Use one general model for every path:

1. **Selection** — Is this the credential I want to pursue?
2. **Registration** — After reviewing current terms, am I ready to make the financial commitment?
3. **Scheduling** — Does my readiness evidence justify choosing an exam date?

These decisions can happen months apart. Path A may select PTCA now. Path B may record “cloud role credential—unselected” until Chapter 12. Path C may record “production or cloud-native milestone—unselected” until Chapter 13.

Selection

Selection follows the work you want to perform and the evidence gap you want to reduce. A useful selection statement is specific:

> This credential matches my chosen path, validates a scope relevant to my target work, and complements the project evidence I am building.

A weak selection statement depends on popularity, a temporary discount, or the hope that payment will manufacture commitment.

Record your current state:

Target credential type: ______

Selection status:

- [ ] Selected
- [ ] Not selected yet
- [ ] No certification currently needed

Next decision point: __________

If you are on Path B, the expected decision point is Chapter 12. If you are on Path C, it is Chapter 13. Do not treat that wait as lost time; build the evidence required to make the later choice honestly.

Registration

Registration is the financial and contractual decision. Before it, verify the current official scope, status, eligibility period, price, tax treatment, cancellation or refund policy, retake policy, identification requirements, and delivery conditions that matter to you.

Do not rely on printed figures or memories of an older exam. Do not interpret a preparation provider's page as proof that a certification is still active. Start with the official certification owner.

Registration can create a useful boundary, but only after selection. It does not itself create readiness.

Scheduling

Scheduling turns readiness into a date. It should follow evidence: practice results, completed objectives, hands-on work, and enough calendar capacity to close the remaining gaps.

Registration and scheduling are not synonyms. A provider may permit them at different times, and policies vary. The durable principle is to schedule when your evidence supports the date—not merely when anxiety demands certainty.

Estimate capacity honestly

Plan from a normal week. Count hours that can survive work, family responsibilities, rest, and disruptions. Four protected hours are more credible than twelve imaginary ones.

Include three kinds of activity:

- concept study, to understand and connect ideas;
- hands-on practice, to retrieve and apply ideas without copying;
- project work, to make decisions in a less controlled setting.

A plan made only of reading and video is not an engineering preparation plan.

Path A quick commitment check

Use this short check only if Chapter 7 produced Decision A.

- [ ] PTCA is genuinely my selected target.
- [ ] I have realistic preparation capacity.
- [ ] I will verify the current official eligibility, refund, retake, and registration terms before making a financial commitment.

If any box remains empty, use Route B below. You lose none of the book's value by waiting.

Ready to review registration?

OPTIONAL RESOURCE

Current PTCA Registration Options

For readers who already selected PTCA, review the current registration requirements, official policies, eligibility information, and alternatives. If you are not ready, save the page and return when the decision becomes relevant.

Review current registration options

www.practicalnotebook.com/the-ai-engineer-roadmap/certification/path-a

My Certification Commitment

Complete the full worksheet after the quick check, whether your status is selected, delayed, or no certification needed.

Target role:

Chosen path:

Target credential type:

Specific credential, if selected:

Why this milestone fits—or why I am waiting:

Selection status:

Registration status:

Scheduling status or target exam month:

Weekly hours available in a normal week:

Hands-on evidence required before the next decision:

First project deadline:

Weakest relevant skill:

Next decision point and date:

Route A — Selected and ready to act

Use Route A only after genuine selection, a current policy review, an acceptable financial decision, and a preparation plan that fits the applicable conditions.

After any registration, return to this book. Record the status, protect the distinction between registration and scheduling, and begin the next project milestone. The purchase is not the finish line.

Route B — Not ready to purchase

Route B is a complete decision. Replace vague delay with evidence requirements and a review date.

My decision date: ______

Before that date, I will complete:

- **Foundation evidence:** ______
- **Path-specific hands-on evidence:** ______
- **Project milestone:** ______
- **Current-policy review:** ______
- **Budget decision:** ______

On that date, choose one action: select and register; define one justified prerequisite; choose another milestone; or remove certification from the current plan.

Do not move the date simply because the decision feels uncomfortable. Move it only when new evidence changes the plan or a named prerequisite could not reasonably be completed.

Make the first milestone small and real

A first milestone should be observable within a short period. Depending on your path, it might be:

- trace and modify a PyTorch training workflow;
- build and evaluate a small model-enabled application;
- containerize and operate a small service;
- create an evaluation plan and reproduce a baseline;
- protect three study blocks during a normal week.

"Study AI" and "work on certification" are not milestones. They have no finish condition.

Protect the return to engineering

Certification study can narrow into recognition of exam-shaped terms. Projects expose whether you can make choices, diagnose failures, and explain limitations.

Your certification plan and project plan should reinforce each other. When study exposes a weak concept, use the project to test it. When a project reveals a gap, update the preparation plan. Do not maintain separate worlds called "exam study" and "real engineering."

The next part returns every path to artifacts:

- Path A builds a reproducible model workflow;
- Path B builds a model-enabled application with evaluation;

- Path C builds a deployable, observable service.

Commitment review

- [ ] My target follows my role and path.
- [ ] I separated selection, registration, and scheduling.
- [ ] I can explain what the milestone may signal and what it cannot prove.
- [ ] My weekly capacity exists in a normal calendar.
- [ ] My plan includes hands-on practice and project work.
- [ ] I recorded a next decision point.
- [ ] If I used Route A, I reviewed current official policies before purchase.
- [ ] If I used Route B, I set evidence requirements and a decision date.
- [ ] I can continue building with official and free resources.

Next step

Place the commitment sheet where you will see it. Reserve the first work block and record one project milestone on your calendar.

> A credential may mark part of the path. The project proves that you can move along it.

CHAPTER 9

Project 1: From Data to Model

Project 1 is the first portfolio artifact in the roadmap. Its purpose is not to make a score appear on a screen. Its purpose is to show that you can take a defined decision, turn it into a measurable prediction problem, build a reproducible baseline, evaluate a model honestly, and explain what the evidence does not establish.

The project is aligned primarily with Path A, but every reader should complete it. A cloud application engineer needs to understand what a model output means before integrating one. A production engineer needs to understand the artifact and lifecycle being deployed. You may use a different domain, but keep the project shape: a bounded prediction task with non-sensitive or synthetic data, a clear baseline, a meaningful evaluation, and a documented failure analysis.

Use a fictional equipment-support operation as the common thread for the three projects. The operation receives maintenance requests for ordinary, non-safety-critical devices. Each request contains a short description, structured fields, and a historical outcome such as whether specialist review was needed.

The project question is:

> Given information available when a request is first received, can a model help triage which requests deserve specialist review?

This is narrower than "build an AI support system." It does not authorize automatic denial, safety decisions, or customer treatment. A model output is advisory and must be reviewed. You can create a synthetic dataset that follows this structure, or use a permitted public dataset with a documented transformation. Do not copy private tickets into a public repository.

Choose a problem that can be explained

Write the project contract before coding:

- the unit is one incoming request;

- the prediction moment is initial intake;
- the target is a historical review outcome defined in the data documentation;
- the action is prioritizing a queue for human review;
- the cost of a missed specialist request is considered separately from the cost of an extra review;
- the model is not the sole decision-maker.

If the historical outcome is a poor proxy for the action you actually care about, say so. A model can be technically accurate and still learn a process artifact.

Requirements and constraints

A credible project starts with constraints rather than an algorithm list.

Record the user of the output, the expected response time, fields present at intake, fields that become available only after review, the privacy boundary, the human override, failure costs, reproducibility commands, and a removal condition. A removal condition might be a new device category, a major process change, or a period in which the labels are no longer comparable.

Put these constraints in the README. They are part of the system design.

Build the data contract

Create a data dictionary with one entry per feature. State its type, allowed values, source, availability at prediction time, missing-value behavior, and whether it is used by the model.

A timestamp may be useful for a time-based split but should not automatically be turned into a meaningless numeric feature. A request category may need a stable mapping. A free-text description may contain identifiers or reveal the target indirectly. Start with structured fields so that the first experiment can be inspected.

Before splitting, remove exact duplicates and investigate records that share an underlying request or customer. If the same incident appears in both training and test data, the model may memorize a pattern rather than learn a general relationship. If time matters, split by time. If one entity contributes many examples, consider a group-aware split.

Never silently discard missing rows. Missingness may signal a process difference. Decide whether to impute, add a missing indicator, reject the row, or include a "not recorded" category. Document the choice and test it.

Establish the baseline

A baseline can be a rule such as "send every request with a known specialist category to review," a majority-class prediction, or a simple linear model. Choose one that a reasonable team could understand and operate.

The baseline report should include the same main metric and test context as the model. For an imbalanced target, include the positive-class rate and a confusion matrix. If the cost of missed review is high, report recall and the number of additional reviews created by a threshold.

Do not hide an unhelpful baseline because it makes the model look better. The baseline tells the reader what a small model has to beat to be useful.

Create the first pipeline

Keep the pipeline in visible stages:

1. load a permitted fixture;
2. validate the schema;
3. split according to the project contract;
4. fit preprocessing on training data only;
5. train the baseline;
6. train one simple model;

7. evaluate on validation data;
8. inspect errors;
9. reserve the final test evaluation for the settled pipeline;
10. save configuration, metrics, and model state.

Use one configuration object or file for feature names, split rules, seed, model settings, threshold, and output directory. A configuration should not contain secrets.

Your first model does not need deep learning. A linear classifier, small tree-based model, or other understandable baseline can reveal whether the feature set contains signal. Path A readers may later implement the same task with a PyTorch model. The comparison is more useful when the data and split remain constant.

Evaluate by decision consequence

Report a small set of metrics that answer the project question. At minimum, report positive-class prevalence, baseline result, chosen operating threshold, precision and recall or an equivalent pair tied to the queue decision, number of requests sent to review, and the largest error groups.

If you use a probability threshold, choose it on validation data or through an explicitly defined cross-validation procedure. Lock it before the final test evaluation.

Separate model quality from queue capacity. A threshold that finds more positives may overwhelm the specialist team. A threshold that reduces review volume may miss cases. The correct operating point is a sociotechnical decision, not a property of the model alone.

Failure analysis

Read at least twenty errors or a defensible sample if the test set is smaller. Use a redacted representation. Group errors by a reason you can investigate rather than by an arbitrary row number.

Useful categories include incomplete intake fields, unfamiliar device category, ambiguous request language, inconsistent historical outcome, a process change, a group with little training data, or a case where the target is not observable from intake information.

For each category, write whether the next action is data repair, feature redesign, threshold review, additional human guidance, or a decision not to use the model there. "Improve the model" is not a sufficient next action.

If a group has poor performance, do not bury it in an average. Explain whether the problem is coverage, label quality, representation, or a different operational process. Avoid claiming fairness or safety from one small analysis.

Reproducibility package

A portfolio reviewer should be able to distinguish a real experiment from a screenshot. Include a README with the decision and limitations, a data dictionary and licensing note, a script that creates or loads the permitted fixture, a clean setup command, training and evaluation commands, configuration, metrics, a confusion matrix or similarly interpretable diagnostic, an error-analysis note, a saved model or documented regeneration command, a test for the inference contract, and a commit history that shows the project evolving.

A large binary model file is not automatically evidence of quality. A small model with a clear evaluation and honest failure analysis is easier to trust.

Portfolio narrative

Write the project as a sequence of decisions:

> The intake team needed a way to prioritize specialist review without changing the final human decision. I defined the prediction moment, removed post-review fields, used a time-aware split, compared a rule baseline with a simple

> model, selected a threshold using validation data, and found that incomplete intake fields dominated the largest error group. The next improvement is a data-collection change, not a larger model.

This paragraph demonstrates judgment. It does not claim the model is ready for production or that the project equals professional experience.

Experiment log and review rhythm

Keep an experiment log that makes each change comparable. Give every run an identifier, a hypothesis, a data or split version, configuration reference, result, and conclusion. Add a "keep, revert, or investigate" decision. The log can be a Markdown file or a small structured dataset; it should not depend on your memory.

Review the log after three or four runs. Look for changes that improved the metric but weakened an important error group, changes that improved training behavior without improving held-out behavior, and changes that added complexity without reducing uncertainty. Stop a line of experimentation when it no longer answers a useful question.

If a result is surprising, reproduce it before explaining it. Check that the command used the intended configuration and split. Check that an output file was not accidentally reused. Check that the metric code matches the written definition. Reproducibility is not only for a final portfolio; it is how you protect your own reasoning while the project is changing.

Alternative domains without losing the shape

You may adapt Project 1 to a different non-sensitive domain: forecasting demand for a fictional inventory system, classifying a permitted set of messages, estimating a measurable numeric outcome, or detecting anomalies in synthetic device telemetry. The domain should not force you to make clinical, legal, financial, or safety-critical decisions from a toy dataset.

When adapting the domain, preserve the structure:

- write the prediction moment;
- document the label source;
- define what happens when the model is uncertain;
- choose a baseline a human could understand;
- inspect errors in meaningful groups;
- record what would have to change before real use.

Changing the domain should change the questions and constraints, not remove the evidence discipline. A portfolio reviewer learns more from a modest project with an honest contract than from a dramatic domain with undefined consequences.

A practical data-split review

Before trusting the first score, write three possible ways the split could lie. Examples include the same request appearing twice, future information encoded in a status field, or a customer or device appearing on both sides. Test each possibility with a query, a group identifier, or a time comparison.

Then compare two plausible splits if the project allows it. A random split may estimate interpolation among similar records; a time split may estimate future use. Neither is automatically correct. The project should explain which question each split answers and which one controls the decision.

Keep the rejected split in the experiment log. A reviewer can then see that the final result was not selected merely because it was favorable.

Path A extension

Path A readers may implement a PyTorch version after the Chapter 6 lab. Keep the same target, split, baseline, and evaluation contract. Add an annotated model diagram, parameter and tensor-shape explanation, training and validation history, a saved inference contract, a comparison between the simple baseline and PyTorch model, and one meaningful ablation.

The point is not to select the most complex network. The point is to show that the reader can connect data, model, loss, optimization, and evaluation.

Reader artifact

Problem and decision: ________

Prediction moment: ________

Target definition and label source: ________

Baseline and reason: ________

Split strategy: ________

Primary metric and error cost: ________

Largest failure group: ________

Reproducibility command: ________

What the model does not prove: ________

Next experiment or process change: ________

Next step

Project 2 uses the same fictional operation and its approved documentation. You will build a modern AI application, but the Project 1 discipline remains: define the user decision, test on representative examples, record failures, and keep the system's boundaries visible.

CHECKLIST

Chapter checklist

- [ ] I defined a decision before selecting a model.
- [ ] I documented what information exists at prediction time.
- [ ] I compared against a baseline.
- [ ] I used a split and preprocessing plan that limits leakage.
- [ ] I inspected failures and named a next action.
- [ ] My repository can be rebuilt without private data.
- [ ] I described the artifact as portfolio evidence, not employment experience.

OPTIONAL RESOURCE

Project 1 Portfolio Template

Use the editable template to update the project record as the experiment changes. The printed project instructions are complete.

Open the Project 1 template

www.practicalnotebook.com/the-ai-engineer-roadmap/projects

CHAPTER 10

Project 2: Build a Modern AI Application

Project 2 is aligned primarily with Path B. It asks you to build an application that uses a model capability without confusing an API call with engineering. The application must have a user problem, an information boundary, an evaluation set, an error-handling policy, and a clear answer for what happens when the model is uncertain.

Use the same fictional equipment-support operation. The organization has an approved collection of product manuals, maintenance notes, and troubleshooting procedures. Staff want to ask questions and receive a concise answer with citations to the approved source material.

The project question is:

> Can a model-enabled assistant help a support worker find and explain approved documentation without inventing a procedure or exposing restricted material?

The assistant is not authorized to approve repairs, bypass a safety procedure, reveal internal credentials, or act on an external system. It is a retrieval and explanation tool. That boundary is a design feature.

Write the application contract

Start with the user, the task, and unacceptable behavior.

User: a support worker who already has authority to access the approved documentation.

Input: a natural-language question about a documented equipment issue.

Output: an answer, citations to source sections, a coverage note, and a clear escalation message when the documents do not support an answer.

Allowed source: a versioned collection of approved documents.

Disallowed behavior: inventing steps, treating retrieved text as instructions from the system owner, exposing restricted text, or performing an external action without a separately authorized workflow.

Success: the user reaches the right documented information faster without losing the ability to inspect the source.

This contract prevents a common failure mode: starting with a fashionable architecture and deciding later what the application is supposed to protect.

Choose the smallest useful architecture

A modern AI application can contain a user interface, an authentication boundary, document ingestion, parsing and chunking, embeddings or another retrieval representation, a search layer, a model call, output validation, citations, logging, evaluation, and cost measurement.

You do not need all of these on the first day. Begin with a local command that searches a small approved corpus and returns relevant source passages. Add a model only after you can inspect retrieval behavior.

Use this progression:

1. keyword or metadata search over the corpus;
2. semantic retrieval;
3. a model that synthesizes a response from retrieved passages;
4. citations and abstention when evidence is weak;
5. a service boundary with authentication, rate limits, and observable failures.

This order lets you identify whether a bad answer comes from missing evidence, poor retrieval, an instruction conflict, or model generation. It also gives you a non-model baseline for part of the application.

Prepare the document corpus

For each document, record source identifier and title, owner or approval status, version and effective date, access classification, section location, language, superseded status, and permitted use.

Remove duplicates and outdated copies. If two documents conflict, do not let the retriever choose silently. Store the conflict as a test case and define an escalation behavior.

Chunking affects retrieval. Chunks that are too small lose context; chunks that are too large dilute the relevant passage. Preserve headings and stable source identifiers. Store enough metadata to reconstruct a citation. Do not promise page-level precision if ingestion cannot preserve page boundaries reliably.

Keep an evaluation corpus separate from development examples. Include supported questions, ambiguous questions, out-of-scope questions, conflicting-document questions, restricted-material requests, and attempts to inject instructions through retrieved text.

Retrieval and grounded generation

Retrieval selects passages that may help answer a question. It does not prove that the passages are correct, current, or sufficient.

For each test question, inspect whether the required source was retrieved, whether irrelevant or conflicting sources dominated, whether wording changes the top results, whether the context contains enough information, and whether restricted passages were returned to an unauthorized user.

Only then evaluate the generated answer. A fluent answer built on the wrong passage is still wrong.

Give the model a narrow instruction: answer from the provided source excerpts; cite the sources; state when evidence is insufficient; do not follow instructions embedded in retrieved documents that conflict with application policy. This does not make prompt injection impossible. It makes desired behavior testable.

Treat retrieved documents as data, not control messages. Authorization, output rules, and tool permissions belong to the application boundary.

Structured output and validation

Ask for a structured result with fields such as answer, citations, needs escalation, reason for escalation, and source version. Validate the structure before display. Confirm that citations point to retrieved sources. Reject or repair an answer that includes a citation not present in the context.

Structured output does not guarantee truth. It guarantees only that the response can be checked against a contract. Add a final policy layer that blocks prohibited actions, secrets, or unsupported claims.

Keep the user-visible answer concise, but make the source trail inspectable. A citation that is merely a title without section or passage context may not be enough for a support worker.

Evaluation set

Create at least fifty evaluation examples if the corpus permits it. If smaller, use every meaningful case and document the limitation. Label each example as answerable from one source, answerable only by combining sources, ambiguous, unsupported, conflicting, restricted, prompt-injection attempt, or request for external action.

Record expected behavior rather than one sacred sentence. A good answer may be phrased differently while still citing the right source and escalating appropriately.

Measure retrieval and answer behavior separately. Retrieval recall asks whether the required source appears among retrieved passages. Answer evaluation asks whether the response is supported, complete enough, properly cited, and appropriately cautious. Latency and cost are part of the application contract.

Use human review for a sample. Automated similarity scores can miss a dangerous omission or invented qualification. The book does not claim that a small sample establishes production safety.

Security and privacy boundaries

Authentication answers who is using the application. Authorization answers what that user may access. A valid login does not authorize every document.

Do not put secrets in prompts or logs. Redact personal identifiers before sending data to an external model when permitted. Set retention rules for questions, retrieved passages, outputs, and traces. Record the minimum information needed to debug.

Treat user input, retrieved text, tool output, and model output as different trust classes. A tool result should not automatically become an instruction. A model output should not automatically trigger an external write. Validate URLs, file paths, and commands at the application boundary.

Set limits for request size, retrieval count, output length, retries, and cost. Rate limiting is part of reliability. A system that can be made to spend unlimited tokens through repetition is not ready for routine use.

Build a threat and trust map

Draw the application as trust zones rather than as a collection of boxes. Mark the public request boundary, authenticated user, authorization service, document store, retrieval index, model provider, logs, and any operator tools. For each arrow, write what crosses it and which component is allowed to initiate the exchange.

This makes several risks visible. A document index may contain content that a user can search but not copy in full. A model provider may receive retrieved passages that require a different retention decision from the original documents. An operator dashboard may contain sensitive timing or error information even if it does not display the answer text. A tool that can write to another system should never be reachable solely because a model proposed a function call.

For every trust boundary, record authentication, authorization, validation, logging, and failure behavior. “The model will not do that” is not a boundary. The application must enforce the decision outside the model.

Compare retrieval methods deliberately

Start with a lexical baseline when the corpus contains distinctive terms, part numbers, or procedure names. Add semantic retrieval when wording variation prevents useful matches. Hybrid retrieval can combine both, but it also adds configuration and debugging paths.

Measure a retrieval change using the same labeled questions. Report whether the required passage appeared, how many irrelevant passages were added, and how latency changed. Do not evaluate only the final answer; otherwise a generation model may hide a retrieval regression by guessing from general knowledge.

Keep a small set of adversarial retrieval cases: a query with a near-synonym, a part number with punctuation, a question that should match two documents, a superseded document, and a restricted document. The point is not to create a perfect benchmark. It is to make the retrieval contract concrete enough to improve.

Cost is part of the feature contract

Record the cost drivers: input length, retrieved context, output length, model selection, embedding or indexing work, storage, and request volume. A local prototype may have no invoice, but it still has a future cost shape.

Set an upper bound for a normal request and a separate behavior for a request that would exceed it. Truncate or summarize only when the evidence contract remains valid. Never silently remove the passage that contains a required qualification just to save tokens.

Cache only when the freshness and authorization rules allow it. A response cached for one user may not be safe to reuse for another. A cached answer may outlive the document version it cites. Include corpus or source-version context in the cache key when caching is appropriate.

Failure analysis

Create a failure log with input and retrieved context, failure class, impact, likely cause, and next experiment. Classes include retrieval miss, unsupported answer, citation error, policy violation, latency, cost, or authorization issue.

Do not patch the prompt after every failure without recording the hypothesis. A longer prompt may hide a retrieval problem and increase cost. A larger model may make a weak citation look fluent without improving evidence.

Fallbacks are product decisions

Design the response when each dependency is unavailable. If the retrieval index is unavailable, should the application return no answer, use a small local index, or direct the user to the source library? If the model provider times out, can the user see retrieved passages with a clear note that synthesis is unavailable? If the authorization service cannot confirm access, should the request fail closed?

Write these choices before testing outages. A fallback that silently weakens authorization or removes citations is not a safe fallback. A fallback that is honest about reduced capability may be more useful than a degraded answer.

Test the boundary with fixtures, not real private records. The test should assert the user-visible behavior, the status or error category, and the fact that sensitive content is not written to the log. This turns an intention into something the application can protect during refactoring.

Human review of an evaluation set

For each reviewed answer, ask three separate questions: Did the system retrieve the needed evidence? Did the answer stay within that evidence? Did it communicate uncertainty and citation clearly enough for the user to act appropriately?

A reviewer may mark an answer "supported but incomplete," "complete but poorly cited," or "appropriately abstained." These categories are more informative than a single pass/fail label. Record disagreements and revise the rubric before changing the model. Otherwise the evaluation set becomes a record of shifting preferences rather than a stable measurement.

Portfolio evidence

A credible Project 2 repository includes a short architecture diagram, source-ingestion decision, corpus manifest, retrieval baseline, model-enabled path, structured output contract, evaluation set, correct-abstention examples, prompt-injection test, authorization test, latency and cost observations, README limitations, and a local-service command.

The project is stronger when you can show a failure, explain why it occurred, and demonstrate the change that reduced it. It is weaker when the README only claims that the assistant is "smart."

Cloud decision preparation

Extract requirements before comparing clouds: model access, object storage, document ingestion, search, identity, secrets management, observability, deployment, scaling, regional constraints, budget, and cost visibility.

Then compare how one cloud would satisfy them. A cloud choice is a set of tradeoffs, not a loyalty declaration. Chapter 12 applies the formal Path B gate after this evidence exists.

Reader artifact

Application problem and user: _____

Approved corpus and access rule: _________

Retrieval baseline: __________

Answer and abstention contract: __________

Evaluation categories: _______

Largest failure class: _______

Security or privacy boundary: ______

Latency/cost observation: __________

Cloud requirement I can now compare: _____

Next step

Project 3 turns this application into an operational system. The purpose is not to add infrastructure for status. It is to make deployment, observability, reproducibility, security, and failure recovery explicit enough that another engineer can reason about the service.

CHECKLIST

Chapter checklist

- [ ] I defined a user task and an unacceptable behavior.
- [ ] I can inspect retrieval separately from generated answers.
- [ ] My application distinguishes data from instructions.
- [ ] I documented authentication and authorization boundaries.
- [ ] I included unsupported, conflicting, restricted, and injection cases.
- [ ] I validate structure and citations before display.
- [ ] I recorded latency, cost, and retention considerations.
- [ ] I can name the cloud requirements that Chapter 12 will compare.

OPTIONAL RESOURCE

Project 2 Portfolio Template

Use the editable template to keep the corpus manifest, evaluation cases, failure log, and architecture decisions together. The project can be completed with local tools and official documentation.

Open the Project 2 template

www.practicalnotebook.com/the-ai-engineer-roadmap/projects

CHAPTER 11

Project 3: Build With Production Constraints

Project 3 is aligned primarily with Path C. It takes the assistant from Chapter 10 and asks a harder question: can another engineer deploy, inspect, reproduce, and recover the service without relying on your memory or a development laptop?

The project is not a claim that a local prototype is production-ready. It is a controlled demonstration of production reasoning. You will define a service boundary, containerize it, record configuration, expose useful health and readiness behavior, log important events without leaking private content, measure latency and cost, and document a failure and recovery path.

The same fictional equipment-support operation remains the domain. The service answers questions from the approved documentation corpus. It does not make repair decisions or write to an external system.

Define the service boundary

Write down what the service does and does not do.

It accepts an authenticated request containing a question and an allowed corpus scope. It retrieves approved passages, calls a model-enabled answer component, validates the structured result, and returns an answer with citations or an escalation response.

It does not accept arbitrary file paths, execute user-provided commands, write to a maintenance database, change permissions, or treat the model output as an authorization decision. If a future product needs one of those behaviors, it requires a separate threat model, interface, permission, and test.

A service boundary is more than a web route. It includes timeouts, request-size limits, authentication, authorization, error responses, logs, metrics, secrets, and a clear owner for each dependency.

Map the lifecycle

Draw the request lifecycle from entry to response:

1. request arrives at the edge;
2. authentication is checked;
3. authorization determines the corpus scope;
4. input is validated;
5. retrieval searches the allowed corpus;
6. the model call runs within a timeout and budget;
7. output structure and citations are checked;
8. the response is returned;
9. selected measurements are recorded;
10. failures are routed to an operator or a safe fallback.

For every step, record one dependency and one failure behavior. If the model provider is unavailable, the service might return a documented temporary-unavailable response rather than fabricate an answer. If retrieval returns no adequate source, the service might ask the user to escalate rather than produce a plausible paragraph.

Containerize for repeatability

Create a container image that can run the service without copying your local machine's hidden state. Use a small base appropriate to the application, install only the required dependencies, and run as a non-root user when the environment permits.

A container image should not contain credentials, private documents, development caches, test dumps, or a source-control directory. Pass configuration through the runtime environment or a secret-management binding. Make the image build observable: record the base image reference, dependency lock or installation method, build command, and resulting version identifier.

Separate build-time and runtime concerns. A build stage can compile or prepare dependencies; the runtime image should contain only what the service needs to start. Do not optimize the image so aggressively that a future maintainer cannot explain it.

Test the image from a clean machine or isolated environment. "It worked inside the development directory" is not a container test.

Configuration and secrets

Separate configuration from code. Configuration might include document index location, maximum retrieved passages, timeout, model identifier, feature flags, and log level. Secrets include API keys, tokens, certificates, and credentials. They require a different handling path.

The README should explain which values are required, which have safe development defaults, and which must be supplied by a secret manager. A sample environment file may contain names and placeholder values but never real credentials.

If a secret enters Git history, assume it is exposed. Revoke or rotate it first. History rewriting may reduce future exposure but cannot erase every clone or cached reference. The safe response is an operational one, not a search-and-replace exercise.

Health, readiness, and dependency behavior

A process can be alive but unable to serve useful traffic. Separate a lightweight liveness signal from readiness.

A liveness check should answer whether the process is responsive. A readiness check can verify essential local initialization and, where appropriate, a dependency condition. Avoid making readiness depend on a slow or billable model call on every probe. If the model provider is unavailable, the service can remain alive while returning a controlled dependency error.

Use timeouts for network calls. Retries should be limited and safe. Retrying a read-only model request may be reasonable under a narrow policy; retrying an operation that could create an external side effect would require idempotency and a different design. This project has no external write action by design.

Observability without surveillance

Logs, metrics, and traces should help an operator answer what happened, how often, and where the system is slow. They should not become a second database of private support questions.

Prefer a request identifier that is random and non-semantic. Record timestamps, route, status class, latency, retrieval count, model response class, and an error category. Do not log raw questions, full retrieved passages, API keys, or unredacted user data by default.

Useful metrics include request count, error count, latency percentiles, retrieval-empty rate, citation-validation failures, model timeout rate, token or usage estimates, and cost per successful response. Define which metrics are estimates and which come directly from a provider response.

Set retention periods. Debug mode should be explicit, short-lived, access-controlled, and reviewed. A portfolio project should demonstrate that it knows the difference between useful diagnostics and unnecessary collection.

Reproducibility and release records

A production-shaped project needs a release record. For each version, store:

- source revision;
- container image identifier;
- dependency and runtime versions;
- configuration reference;

- corpus version;
- model or provider identifier;
- evaluation report;
- known limitations;
- rollback instruction.

A model-enabled service can change behavior when the corpus, embedding model, prompt, provider model, threshold, or dependency changes. A version string that tracks only application code is not enough.

Run the evaluation suite before a release. Compare retrieval, answer support, abstention, latency, and cost to the previous record. A release can be rejected because answer quality is unchanged but latency or cost violates the project constraint.

Failure drill

Write a failure drill in the README and rehearse it locally:

Case: the model provider begins returning timeouts.

Detection: model-timeout metric exceeds the defined threshold and logs show the dependency error.

Immediate behavior: return a clear temporary-unavailable response or a retrieval-only fallback that does not pretend to answer.

Operator action: check provider status, recent configuration changes, and request volume; prevent unbounded retries.

Recovery: restore the previous working configuration or provider route, rerun a smoke test and a representative evaluation sample, then record the incident.

Learning: decide whether timeout, budget, cache, fallback, or user-facing messaging should change.

Create a second drill for a bad corpus release. Roll back to the previous corpus version and verify that citations return to known documents. Do not make "restart the container" the entire recovery plan.

Deployment choices

You can run the service locally, on a single managed container, or on a small cloud service. Choose the simplest environment that lets you demonstrate the lifecycle. Kubernetes is not required for a single service and should not be added merely to make the diagram look advanced.

If you deploy to a cloud, document identity, network exposure, storage, secrets, logs, cost controls, and deletion steps. Avoid leaving an expensive or publicly exposed resource running after the exercise. Use least privilege and remove unused resources.

A deployment diagram should show trust boundaries and data movement, not only boxes labeled with product names. Explain why each managed service exists and what you would replace if the budget or data boundary changed.

Capacity and cost envelope

Write down the service envelope before trying to scale it. Estimate ordinary request volume, peak bursts, maximum acceptable latency, maximum retrieval size, model usage, storage, and log retention. State which values are measured and which are assumptions.

A small service can fail economically before it fails technically. A retry storm, an oversized request, a verbose model response, or an accidentally enabled debug trace can multiply cost. Add a budget limit, a request limit, and an operator alert. A limit that produces a clear refusal is safer than a system that quietly spends until an invoice arrives.

Deployment levels

Describe three levels in the project record. Level one is a local container that another person can run. Level two is a short-lived managed deployment with controlled access, logs, cost limits, and a deletion plan. Level three would add stronger availability, release automation, dependency redundancy, and incident ownership.

You do not need to implement every level. Naming the missing controls prevents a local demonstration from being mistaken for a production service. It also gives an interviewer a precise answer when asked what you would do next.

For each level, record the new failure modes. A managed deployment may add identity configuration, network exposure, region, provider quota, and billing. It may reduce some host-maintenance work while increasing the importance of access policy and provider-specific monitoring. Architecture is a tradeoff record, not a list of services.

If you compare a local and cloud run, keep the workload and evaluation set stable. Record cold-start behavior separately from warm-request behavior. Do not compare a developer laptop with a production guarantee. The value of the exercise is learning which measurements the next deployment must collect.

Runbook quality test

Give the README to a person who did not build the service. Ask them to perform five actions without oral help: start it, make a valid request, make an invalid request, inspect a failure, and roll back to the previous release record.

Watch where they hesitate. If they need a private shell alias, undocumented environment variable, or knowledge of your directory structure, the runbook is incomplete. Fix the document and repeat the test. Documentation is operational behavior made visible.

Add an ownership line to each major failure: who decides whether to disable the model route, who restores the previous corpus, who confirms that an incident is closed, and where the decision is recorded. A system with no named decision owner can remain broken while every component appears healthy.

Production artifact

The Project 3 repository should contain the container build, local run command, configuration example, health and readiness behavior, structured logs, a small metric set, evaluation command, release record, failure drills, rollback instruction, threat notes, and a README that states what is not production-ready.

Show one controlled failure. A service that never fails in a demo has not demonstrated resilience. A service that fails and recovers with a documented, safe path demonstrates more.

Reader artifact

Service boundary: __________

Input, output, and refusal behavior: _____

Container build and run command: _______

Secret and configuration boundary: ______

Health/readiness distinction: _____

Key metrics and retention rule: ________

Release record fields: ______

Failure drill and recovery: _______

Rollback target: __________

What remains out of scope: _______

Next step

Chapter 12 helps Path B readers choose one cloud ecosystem after application evidence exists. Chapter 13 helps Path C readers decide which production milestone, if any, matches the system work they can now explain.

CHECKLIST

Chapter checklist

- [ ] I defined a service boundary and excluded unsafe external actions.
- [ ] I can build and run the service from a clean environment.
- [ ] Configuration and secrets have separate handling paths.
- [ ] Health, readiness, timeouts, and retries are explicit.
- [ ] Logs and metrics avoid unnecessary private data.
- [ ] I recorded the corpus, model, code, and dependency versions.
- [ ] I rehearsed a dependency failure and a rollback.
- [ ] I described the artifact as portfolio evidence, not production experience.

OPTIONAL RESOURCE

Project 3 Portfolio Template

Use the editable template to document the service boundary, container, release record, failure drill, and production limitations. The project can be completed with local tools and official documentation.

Open the Project 3 template

www.practicalnotebook.com/the-ai-engineer-roadmap/projects

CHAPTER 12

Choose a Cloud Without Learning All Three

Cloud choice is an engineering decision with a career consequence. It should follow the application you want to build, the roles you want to pursue, and the constraints you can explain—not the order in which certification advertisements reach you.

This chapter is the Path B decision point. The reader should have an application contract, a retrieval or model-enabled prototype, evaluation cases, and a list of requirements from Chapter 10. If those artifacts do not exist, use the "not yet" route and keep building.

Compare requirements, not logos

Start with the capability categories:

- model access and model lifecycle;
- document and object storage;
- search or retrieval;
- identity and authorization;
- secrets management;
- deployment and scaling;
- logs, metrics, and traces;
- networking and data movement;
- region and data-boundary constraints;
- cost visibility and budget controls;
- support and learning resources.

For each category, state the minimum capability you need and one trade-off. A managed model endpoint may reduce operations work but constrain model choice or pricing. A hosted search service may accelerate a prototype but create a data-migration cost. A managed identity system may improve control while requiring provider-specific knowledge.

Do not compare every product in a catalog. Compare the smallest architecture that can satisfy Project 2 and Project 3 constraints.

Make the comparison inspectable

Use a short decision record rather than a page of product names. For each capability, write the requirement, the candidate service category, one advantage, one tradeoff, and the evidence you used. If the evidence is only a vendor claim, label it as such and identify the test you would run.

Ask which parts of the design are portable. Application interfaces, evaluation cases, document metadata, and authorization rules can often be kept provider-neutral even when the deployment adapter is specific. Ask which parts are intentionally provider-specific, such as a managed model endpoint or identity integration. Portability is a tradeoff with a cost; it is not a moral requirement.

Do not use price calculators as promises. Record the assumptions behind any estimate: region, request volume, storage, model usage, retention, and discounts. A small workload can have a different cost shape from a production workload. The point is to learn which variables control the bill and how to set a limit.

If a cloud comparison produces no clear winner, choose based on the strongest evidence path: the ecosystem your target role uses, the service you can explain, and the project you can complete. An explicit "defer cloud selection until the next experiment" is better than a shallow tour of three dashboards.

Credential research worksheet

When you open an official credential page, capture the access date, owner, current status, audience, scope, delivery method, policy links, and the project evidence that complements it. Capture what the credential does not assess as carefully as what it does.

Then inspect one preparation option only if the credential remains a fit. Compare its update date, scope mapping, lab depth, refund terms, access period, and disclosure requirements. A commercial page can help you find a course, but it cannot override the official owner's status or make a stale course current.

If the current catalog is in transition, record "online verification required" and continue with the project. A dynamic page is useful precisely because it can change without forcing a new printed claim.

Choose one primary ecosystem

Use target work as evidence. Read a sample of job descriptions or talk to people who do the role, then record which capabilities and ecosystems appear repeatedly. Treat job postings as signals, not promises. A provider name appearing in one posting is not enough to define your path.

Also consider transferable learning. An application built with one cloud can teach identity, storage, deployment, monitoring, and cost reasoning that transfer conceptually. The goal is not to become unable to work anywhere else. The goal is to go deep enough in one environment to produce evidence.

Record the decision:

Primary cloud ecosystem: ____________

Target role evidence: ________

Project requirement it satisfies best: _____

Cost or operational constraint: ___________

What I am deliberately not learning yet: _________

If the choice is genuinely uncertain, choose a short comparison experiment with the same small application and a fixed time limit. Do not build three complete versions. Compare one critical workflow and record what changed.

Consult the current credential catalog

Only after selecting a cloud should you inspect its current official credentials. Use the official catalog and credential page as the source of truth. Names, codes, objectives, delivery methods, prices, retirement notices, and preparation recommendations can change.

A credential may fit when its scope matches your target role, the ecosystem appears in your intended work, you have built relevant application evidence, and you can describe what the credential adds beyond the project. It may not fit when it is a foundational survey for a practitioner who needs application depth, when it is being retired, or when its scope is mostly unrelated to your work.

A preparation provider is not the credential owner. Evaluate a course only after you have selected the current credential and compared its syllabus with the official scope. Keep official free resources visible.

Path B decision gate

Make one decision

Decision A — A current cloud credential is my next milestone.

Credential family and official page to verify: ______

Why it fits this work: ________

Evidence I still need beyond the credential: _______

Decision B — I chose a cloud, but certification comes later.

The next application or deployment artifact is: _____

Review date: _______

Decision C — I do not need a cloud certification now.

The project evidence I will build instead: ____

Do not review a credential option before Decision A. Decision B and C are complete outcomes.

CHECKLIST

A current cloud AI credential may fit if

- [ ] I have completed a relevant application artifact.
- [ ] I chose one primary cloud ecosystem.
- [ ] My target roles use or value that ecosystem.
- [ ] I can explain evaluation, security, latency, deployment, and cost tradeoffs.
- [ ] The official credential is active and current.
- [ ] Its scope matches work I want to perform.
- [ ] I understand that the credential does not replace project evidence.

CHECKLIST

Wait if

- [ ] I chose a cloud because it matches the work I want to build and operate.
- [ ] I have not built or evaluated an application.
- [ ] I am trying to learn three ecosystems at once.
- [ ] The credential is being retired or replaced.
- [ ] A foundation gap is the real blocker.
- [ ] I cannot explain what the credential would add.

OPTIONAL RESOURCE

Current Cloud AI Credential Paths

Use this page only after Decision A. Compare the current official catalog, fit criteria, preparation options, and reasons to wait. Keep the official provider page as the source of truth before registering.

Review the current cloud credential paths

www.practicalnotebook.com/the-ai-engineer-roadmap/certification/path-b

Keep the cloud choice reversible enough

A cloud decision is important, but it is not a lifetime identity. Record the assumptions that would cause a review: target roles change, a required region becomes unavailable, costs exceed the project boundary, or the ecosystem no longer supports the application requirement.

Do not hide portability work. Keep application interfaces, configuration, evaluation fixtures, and data contracts separate from provider-specific adapters where reasonable. Portability is not free, but a clear boundary makes future change discussable.

Next step

Path B now returns to the shared preparation framework. Path C readers should continue to Chapter 13 before choosing a production milestone. Everyone should keep building project evidence rather than turning a credential decision into the finish line.

CHECKLIST

Chapter checklist

- [ ] I compared capabilities and constraints rather than brand recognition.
- [ ] I selected one primary cloud ecosystem.
- [ ] I recorded target-role evidence and a project requirement.
- [ ] I consulted the current official credential catalog.
- [ ] I made Decision A, B, or C before reviewing the current credential page.
- [ ] I can continue with official and free resources.

CHAPTER 13

Linux, Containers, Kubernetes, and Your Production Milestone

Production AI work is not a list of fashionable infrastructure nouns. It is the ability to make a system repeatable, deployable, observable, secure, and recoverable under constraints.

This chapter is the Path C decision point. The reader should have Linux and container practice, a small operated service, and the Project 3 lifecycle record. Kubernetes may be relevant, but it is not automatically the next step. A smaller service that you can explain is stronger evidence than an elaborate cluster you copied without understanding.

Start with the smallest production unit

Before orchestration, operate one service. Navigate the host, inspect processes, permissions, environment, ports, and logs. Build and run a container. Change configuration without rebuilding the image. Stop the process and recover it. Record the commands and the expected signals.

The goal is not to become a system administrator in one chapter. It is to understand the state that a platform later has to manage.

A service lifecycle includes code, dependencies, configuration, data, model or provider behavior, logs, metrics, health, deployment, rollback, and ownership. If you cannot describe the lifecycle for one service, adding a cluster increases the number of unknowns.

Reproducibility before orchestration

Make a fresh environment produce the same application shape:

- install or build from a recorded dependency set;
- create a known corpus or fixture;
- run the evaluation;
- start the service;
- issue a test request;
- inspect logs and metrics;
- stop and restart it;

- compare the result with an acceptable variation range.

Version the corpus and configuration. Record model/provider identifiers. Distinguish reproducibility of the code path from exact equality of model outputs. External model behavior can change even when your application code does not.

Understand what Kubernetes adds

Kubernetes is an orchestration system for managing containerized workloads and related resources. Its value appears when scheduling, service discovery, scaling, rollout, isolation, or operational coordination creates a problem a simpler deployment does not solve.

It also introduces concepts that must be understood: desired state, controllers, pods, services, configuration, secrets, health probes, resource requests, limits, namespaces, permissions, and failure behavior. Learning command syntax without these concepts produces fragile demonstrations.

Ask before adopting it:

- What repeated operational problem does orchestration solve?
- How will I observe a failed rollout?
- Which identity can read secrets or deploy workloads?
- What is the rollback target?
- How will cost and capacity be controlled?
- Who owns the cluster and its upgrades?

If you do not have a good answer, a managed single-service deployment or local container project may be the better milestone.

A small Linux and container lab

Use the Project 3 service and perform the same exercise on a clean environment. Inspect the process and listening port. Change one configuration value through the runtime environment. Stop the process and confirm that the health signal changes. Start it again and verify that the service returns to the expected state. Examine the logs for a useful failure category rather than a private payload.

Then build the container from the repository. Run it with a deliberately missing configuration value and record the failure. Add the value through the documented runtime path, not by editing the image. Create a second container with a changed application version and practice identifying which version produced a response.

This lab is small by design. It teaches the state transitions that an orchestrator later automates. If the reader cannot explain why the service stopped, what the health signal means, or where configuration entered, a larger platform will only make the diagnosis slower.

Linux questions worth practicing

Practice explaining a service through questions rather than command memorization. Which process owns the port? Which user owns the files? Which environment values were present at startup? Where did the error appear first? Which log line is an effect rather than a cause? What state survives a restart?

Use safe, read-only inspection first. A production engineer needs to know what a command changes before running it on a shared system. For the portfolio project, record the command family, the expected output, and the limitation of the local simulation. The goal is to build a mental model that transfers, not to collect a list of terminal incantations.

When a credential later tests a broader scope, this foundation helps you decide whether the scope represents a useful next responsibility. It does not mean the small lab has already demonstrated administration of a real cluster.

When a platform milestone is premature

A reader may be technically capable of following a Kubernetes tutorial and still not be ready for an operations credential. Warning signs include a service with no reproducible build, no logs that distinguish failure classes, no rollback target, no understanding of identity, or no reason the workload needs scheduling or scaling.

The answer is not to reject platform engineering permanently. Complete the smallest missing artifact, operate the service again, and revisit the decision. The credential should mark a need that has become understandable, not create an identity that the project has not earned.

Choose the maturity-appropriate category

The Linux Foundation and other credential owners may offer distinct scopes across foundational cloud-native knowledge, Linux administration, Kubernetes application development, Kubernetes operations, and platform engineering. These categories are alternatives, not a mandatory sequence.

A foundational milestone can fit a reader who needs vocabulary and a bounded first step. A Linux administration milestone can fit a role that genuinely operates systems. A Kubernetes application milestone can fit a developer who deploys workloads but does not own cluster operations. An administration milestone can fit a reader responsible for cluster behavior. Platform-engineering milestones belong later when the reader designs or operates shared internal platforms.

The current official catalog decides the exact names, scope, status, policies, and eligibility. The print book provides the reasoning framework.

Path C decision gate

Make one decision

Decision A — One current production milestone is my next step.

Milestone category and official page to verify: _____

Why it fits this work: _____________

Hands-on evidence still required: ______

Decision B — Production direction selected; certification later.

The next operational artifact is: ______

Review date: _________

Decision C — No certification is needed now.

The system evidence I will build instead: _____

CHECKLIST

A production or cloud-native credential may fit if

- [ ] I can operate a small Linux-based service.
- [ ] I can build and inspect a container.
- [ ] I understand logs, configuration, health, failure recovery, and reproducibility.
- [ ] The technology appears in my target work.
- [ ] I can explain the lifecycle the credential validates.
- [ ] The official credential is active and current.
- [ ] I need one milestone now, not a catalog of certifications.

CHECKLIST

Wait if

- [ ] Kubernetes is still only a buzzword to me.
- [ ] I have never containerized and operated a small service.
- [ ] I cannot explain how a failed deployment is detected or rolled back.
- [ ] I am collecting credentials instead of building systems.
- [ ] The credential scope exceeds my practical foundation.
- [ ] My target work does not require the technology.

OPTIONAL RESOURCE

Current Production AI Milestones

Use this page only after Decision A. Compare current Linux, cloud-native, Kubernetes, and platform-engineering options by maturity, hands-on prerequisites, and target work. No certification ladder is implied.

Review the current production milestones

www.practicalnotebook.com/the-ai-engineer-roadmap/certification/path-c

Project and credential remain separate

A credential can organize preparation. Project 3 demonstrates that you can operate a bounded service and explain its tradeoffs. Do not replace the failure drill, release record, or runbook with a badge image.

When a new responsibility appears—shared platform ownership, cluster administration, or reliability at a different scale—revisit the gate. A later milestone is justified by the new work, not by a desire to complete a ladder.

Next step

Chapter 14 creates a twelve-week plan that adapts to your selected path and current constraint. It is a planning template, not a promise that any credential or career transition can be completed in twelve weeks.

CHECKLIST

Chapter checklist

- [ ] I operated one service before considering orchestration.
- [ ] I can explain the production lifecycle and rollback.
- [ ] I understand the difference between application and operations responsibilities.
- [ ] I selected one milestone category or chose later/none.
- [ ] I made the decision before reviewing the current milestone page.
- [ ] I can continue with official documentation and project work without a partner.

CHAPTER 14

Build Your Adaptable 12-Week Preparation Plan

Twelve weeks is a useful planning horizon because it is long enough to produce evidence and short enough to inspect honestly. It is not a promise that a person can become an AI engineer, pass an exam, or change careers in twelve weeks.

The plan should adapt to your path, starting level, available capacity, and current constraint. A reader with six hours per week needs a different sequence from a reader with twenty. A Path A reader may need model and PyTorch practice. A Path B reader may need application architecture and cloud deployment. A Path C reader may need Linux, containers, and operational habits. The framework stays stable while the contents change.

Start with capacity, not ambition

Open a normal calendar. Do not plan from a week with no interruptions.

Record:

Minimum weekly capacity: ____________

Preferred weekly capacity: __________

Protected blocks: _____________

Unreliable periods: ___________

Recovery or buffer block: ___________

A protected block has a location, a start time, a finish time, and a small first action. "Study on Tuesday" is not protected. "Tuesday 19:00–20:00, reproduce the evaluation command and write three observations" is.

Keep at least one buffer block. A plan with no recovery time treats normal life as an exception and turns one missed session into a broken month.

Use five work types

A balanced week includes five kinds of work:

1. **Concept study** connects a new idea to the system you are building.

2. **Hands-on practice** makes you retrieve and use the idea without copying.
3. **Project work** forces choices in a less controlled setting.
4. **Weak-domain repair** removes a specific blocker.
5. **Review and recovery** protects memory, documentation, and the next week's capacity.

Do not spend every hour consuming explanations. When a concept is important, use a short study block, a hands-on exercise, and a project application. If you cannot explain what changed after a week, the plan may be too passive.

A durable weekly template

Use this as a starting point, then adjust the proportions:

Block 1 — concept: one bounded topic and a written explanation.

Block 2 — hands-on: one implementation or debugging task.

Block 3 — project: one artifact that changes the repository or experiment.

Block 4 — review: update the README, metrics, decisions, and next action.

If you have less capacity, alternate concept and hands-on work while protecting one project block. If you have more, add experiments and review before adding more topics.

Write a completion condition for every block. "Read about containers" is not complete. "Build the image, inspect the process, and record one failure mode" is.

Path A adaptation

Path A—AI / ML Engineer with PyTorch—should balance:

- Python and ML concept repair;

- PyTorch tensors, datasets, models, loss, gradients, and evaluation;
- Project 1 data contract, baseline, model, error analysis, and saved artifact;
- selected certification objectives only after the credential has been chosen;
- weak-domain remediation and review.

A sample sequence:

Weeks 1–2: reproduce the data contract and baseline; repair Python or statistics gaps exposed by the project.

Weeks 3–4: implement the PyTorch model and verify shapes, loss, modes, and device behavior.

Weeks 5–6: run a controlled experiment and compare with the baseline.

Weeks 7–8: perform error analysis, improve the inference contract, and test a meaningful modification.

Weeks 9–10: document the project, review selected credential scope if applicable, and identify gaps.

Weeks 11–12: consolidate evidence, run a readiness check, and decide whether to continue, register, schedule later, or choose another milestone.

Do not treat this as an exam syllabus. If no credential is selected, replace the credential block with deeper model evaluation or project explanation.

Path B adaptation

Path B—Cloud AI Application Engineer—should balance:

- application architecture;
- model API and retrieval behavior;
- evaluation, structured output, abstention, and citations;
- identity, security, latency, cost, and deployment;

- one selected cloud ecosystem;
- Project 2 evidence;
- current credential preparation only after the Chapter 12 decision.

A sample sequence:

Weeks 1–2: write the application contract and corpus manifest; build a non-model retrieval baseline.

Weeks 3–4: add model synthesis, structured output, citation validation, and unsupported-question behavior.

Weeks 5–6: create the evaluation set; test retrieval misses, conflicts, restricted content, and instruction injection.

Weeks 7–8: choose one cloud using requirements; deploy the smallest useful service or complete a controlled cloud comparison.

Weeks 9–10: measure latency, cost, authorization behavior, and failure recovery; document the architecture.

Weeks 11–12: complete the Path B credential decision, then either prepare for the selected milestone or keep building without certification.

A cloud credential should not replace the application README, evaluation set, or deployment evidence.

Path C adaptation

Path C—Production AI / MLOps Engineer—should balance:

- Linux and process behavior;
- container construction and runtime configuration;
- deployment and rollback;
- logs, metrics, traces, and safe retention;
- reproducibility and release records;
- orchestration only when relevant;
- Project 3 failure drills;

- selected production credential preparation only after the Chapter 13 decision.

A sample sequence:

Weeks 1–2: operate the service locally; inspect processes, ports, logs, configuration, and permissions.

Weeks 3–4: build and run the container from a clean environment; separate secrets and configuration.

Weeks 5–6: add health/readiness behavior, timeouts, structured logs, and a small metric set.

Weeks 7–8: write and rehearse a dependency failure and rollback; create a release record.

Weeks 9–10: evaluate whether orchestration solves a real constraint; if yes, learn the smallest relevant scope.

Weeks 11–12: complete the Path C milestone decision and either prepare for one selected credential or continue improving the service.

Do not add Kubernetes tasks merely because the calendar has room. Add them only when the project exposes a problem that orchestration can address.

Weak-domain repair

A weak domain should be concrete. "I am bad at math" is not a repair plan. "I cannot explain why a held-out split changes the estimate" is.

Write:

Observed blocker: ______________

Smallest concept needed: ______________

Practice task: __________

Evidence that it improved: ___________

Review date: ____________

If a blocker persists after two attempts, change the explanation, task, or support resource. Do not simply increase the number of hours.

Weekly review

At the end of each week, answer:

- What did I complete?
- What evidence did I create?
- What failed?
- What assumption changed?
- Which task should be removed, not postponed?
- What is the first action of the next block?
- Did the plan leave enough recovery capacity?

A plan is a control system. It should respond to evidence. Changing it is not failure when the reason is documented.

Three sample weeks

Imagine three readers with the same twelve-week horizon.

Reader A has four protected hours and strong software experience but weak ML evaluation. Their first week contains one evaluation study block, one baseline implementation block, one error-analysis block, and a short review. They do not add a cloud course because it would not remove the current blocker.

Reader B has eight hours and can write Python but has never shipped an application. Their first week creates the corpus manifest and a retrieval-only baseline. They postpone certification research until the application can be evaluated and a cloud choice has evidence.

Reader C has six hours and years of systems experience but little model knowledge. Their first week runs the existing service locally, documents the container boundary, and then completes one model-evaluation task. They do not jump to Kubernetes because the missing evidence is not orchestration.

The template is the same; the sequence is different. Capacity planning is useful when it protects the constraint that matters most.

Stop rules for an overloaded plan

Write three stop rules before the twelve weeks begin. For example: stop adding tools when the project has not produced a new evaluation case; stop increasing model size when the baseline comparison is not stable; stop adding infrastructure when the runbook cannot be followed by another person.

Stop rules reduce the pressure to turn every difficulty into a request for more complexity. They also give you a defensible explanation when someone asks why you did not add another framework or certification.

Selecting support without losing ownership

A structured course, book, mentor, or lab can reduce a specific gap. Before choosing one, write the task you cannot yet complete, the evidence that would show improvement, and the maximum time or budget you can devote. Compare the support against official free resources and the project itself.

Do not outsource the decision to a course catalog. A provider may organize lessons well and still be the wrong fit for your current problem. Keep your own project repository, experiment log, and review date outside the provider platform. If the course disappears, your evidence should remain.

Reader artifact

Twelve-week objective: ________

Path: ___________

Weekly capacity: _______

Project artifact due by week 4: __________

Project artifact due by week 8: __________

Final evidence review: ________

Weak-domain repair: _________

Recovery rule: ________

What I will deliberately not learn yet: _________

Next step

Chapter 15 tests readiness for a project milestone, a certification schedule, or a deliberate "not yet." The correct outcome depends on evidence, not on how much money or time has already been spent.

CHECKLIST

Chapter checklist

- [ ] My plan starts with normal weekly capacity.
- [ ] Every week includes concept, hands-on, project, repair, and review/recovery work in a realistic balance.
- [ ] My path changes the content of the plan.
- [ ] Twelve weeks is a planning horizon, not a guarantee.
- [ ] I wrote completion conditions for my first blocks.
- [ ] I recorded what I will not learn yet.

OPTIONAL RESOURCE

Adaptable AI Engineer Study Planner

The printable framework is complete. Scan to move blocks, record evidence, and keep a dated review history.

Open the adaptable study planner

www.practicalnotebook.com/the-ai-engineer-roadmap/study-plan

CHAPTER 15

Know When You Are Ready

Readiness is a claim about a specific action. You can be ready to publish a project README and not ready to schedule an exam. You can be ready to deploy a local service and not ready to promise its reliability to users. You can be ready to select a credential and not ready to sit its assessment.

Use this chapter to make the claim smaller and testable.

Four kinds of readiness

Concept readiness means you can explain the relevant ideas and distinguish a correct-looking result from a misleading one.

Hands-on readiness means you can perform the central tasks without copying every step and can diagnose common failures.

Artifact readiness means your repository, experiment record, or service can be inspected by another person.

Commitment readiness means the calendar, policies, budget, and next decision are realistic.

A credential schedule should require all four at an appropriate level. A project milestone may require strong artifact and hands-on evidence even when concept knowledge is still developing.

Shared readiness gate

Check the statements that are true for your next action:

- [ ] I can state the action I am considering in one sentence.
- [ ] I can name the evidence that supports it.
- [ ] I can name the most likely failure.
- [ ] I have a recovery or next-step plan.
- [ ] I have checked current technical and policy constraints.
- [ ] The action fits a normal calendar.
- [ ] I can continue if no affiliate resource is available.

- [ ] I know what would make me postpone the action.

If fewer than five statements are true, choose a smaller milestone. If the missing statements concern safety, authorization, current policy, or financial commitment, do not schedule until they are resolved.

Path A — model and PyTorch readiness

A Path A reader preparing for a PyTorch credential or a Project 1 milestone should be able to trace a training workflow, explain tensor shapes, use a data split that limits leakage, compare with a baseline, inspect errors, save and reload the inference contract, and describe limitations.

For scheduling a selected Path A credential, also verify the current provider rules, eligibility window, delivery requirements, identification process, rescheduling and retake policy, and any system test. These details belong to the current Practical Notebook page and official provider, not to the permanent print claim.

If readiness is weak, choose one of three actions:

- complete a named PyTorch or evaluation prerequisite;
- schedule a new evidence review date;
- choose a project milestone instead of a credential date.

OPTIONAL RESOURCE

Current Path A Scheduling Policies

If Path A is your selected milestone, scan to verify current eligibility, technical requirements, identification, reservation, and retake information before scheduling.

Check current Path A policies before scheduling

www.practicalnotebook.com/the-ai-engineer-roadmap/certification/path-a

Path B — application and cloud readiness

A Path B reader should be able to explain the application contract, retrieve approved sources, validate citations, handle unsupported questions, protect authorization boundaries, measure latency and cost, and deploy or otherwise reproduce the application in the selected ecosystem.

For scheduling a selected Path B credential, verify the current official scope, delivery method, identification, reservation rules, technical requirements, and policy dates. A preparation course is optional and subordinate to the application evidence.

OPTIONAL RESOURCE

Current Path B Scheduling Policies

If Path B is your selected milestone, scan after choosing one ecosystem and one current credential. Confirm the official scope and scheduling policies before committing.

Check current cloud credential policies

www.practicalnotebook.com/the-ai-engineer-roadmap/certification/path-b

Path C — production readiness

A Path C reader should be able to build and inspect a container, operate a small service, separate configuration and secrets, read logs and metrics, explain a rollback, and identify whether orchestration solves a real constraint.

For scheduling a selected Path C milestone, verify the current official scope, performance or delivery environment, system requirements, identification, reservation, and policy details. Do not schedule a more advanced milestone because a simpler one feels less prestigious.

These three blocks are conditional instructions, not a certification menu. If you have no selected credential, scan none of them. Continue with the project readiness gate.

OPTIONAL RESOURCE

Current Path C Scheduling Policies

If Path C is your selected milestone, scan after choosing one maturity-appropriate target. Confirm the official scope and current policies before committing.

Check current production milestone policies

www.practicalnotebook.com/the-ai-engineer-roadmap/certification/path-c

Schedule, postpone, or remove

Write a decision that can be reviewed:

Action: __________

Evidence already complete: __________

Evidence still missing: _______

Current policy checked on: __________

Target date or review date: _________

Postpone if: ___________

Remove the action if: _________

A postponed exam is not wasted effort if the evidence tells you what to repair. A removed credential is not a failed career plan if the project evidence remains useful.

Readiness is a conversation with evidence

Ask a reviewer to challenge your readiness card. They should be able to ask "How do you know?" and receive a link to a run, metric report, failure log, or policy page. If the only answer is that you studied for a certain number of hours, the card is incomplete.

For a project milestone, ask the reviewer to reproduce one command and inspect one failure. For a credential milestone, ask them to verify that the current official scope and policies were checked. For a deployment milestone, ask them to follow the runbook and perform the rollback.

The reviewer does not need to agree with every decision. Their questions should expose assumptions you can either support, revise, or record as limitations. Readiness grows through this conversation; it is not a feeling you must manufacture alone.

A readiness score is not a grade

You may use a simple three-state record for each requirement: demonstrated, partially demonstrated, or not yet demonstrated. Do not average the states into a single number. One missing safety, authorization, or current-policy requirement can matter more than several completed study tasks.

The record should include evidence links and a next action. "Partially demonstrated" is useful when it points to a test: run the service after a restart, reproduce the split, or explain the loss without notes. The goal is a decision that can change when evidence changes, not a score that creates false precision.

Reader artifact

Complete one readiness card for the next concrete action. Attach the relevant repository, metric report, service runbook, or decision record. Do not attach only a course completion screenshot or a list of topics read.

Next step

Chapter 16 turns these artifacts into a portfolio that explains decisions. A repository does not speak for itself; the reader needs to understand the problem, the tradeoffs, the evidence, and the limits.

CHECKLIST

Chapter checklist

- [ ] I separated concept, hands-on, artifact, and commitment readiness.
- [ ] My next action is specific.
- [ ] I can state what would make me postpone it.
- [ ] I used only the QR block for my selected path, or none if no credential is selected.
- [ ] I verified current policy details online.
- [ ] My evidence remains useful if the credential or affiliate program disappears.

CHAPTER 16

Build a Portfolio That Explains Your Skills

A portfolio is not a storage bin for notebooks. It is a set of evidence packages that help another person understand what you built, why you built it, how you tested it, where it failed, and what you would do next.

The reviewer may spend only a few minutes at first. Your repository must make the important path visible without hiding the detailed evidence deeper in the project.

The evidence package

For each project, create a consistent opening:

1. **Problem:** what user or team needed to decide or accomplish.
2. **Constraints:** data, time, privacy, cost, reliability, or access limits.
3. **Approach:** what you chose and why.
4. **Evaluation:** how you measured behavior.
5. **Failure analysis:** where the system did not work.
6. **Reproducibility:** how another person runs it.
7. **Limitations:** what the evidence cannot establish.
8. **Next experiment:** the smallest useful improvement.

This structure helps a reviewer compare projects without forcing them to guess what each folder means.

The five-minute path

Design a short path for a reviewer who has not met you. The root README should state the target role, link to the three projects, and identify the one artifact to open first. That project README should state the problem, show one result with context, link to the evaluation or runbook, and name one failure.

The reviewer should be able to answer five questions quickly: what was built, why it exists, how it was tested, what went wrong, and what the author would do next. If the answer requires opening ten notebooks, the portfolio is asking the reviewer to become the project manager.

Keep deep evidence available behind the short path. Configuration, raw metrics, logs, diagrams, and experiment history are valuable when a reviewer wants to investigate. They should not obscure the first explanation.

Peer review as a portfolio feature

Ask for review before polishing the repository. Give the reviewer one task: reproduce a result, find a limitation, or challenge a design decision. Record the feedback and your response. You do not need to accept every suggestion; explain why you did or did not change the artifact.

This creates evidence of collaboration without claiming a team role you did not have. It also reveals whether your README communicates enough context for another engineer to contribute.

Keep a change record

For every published project version, record what changed, why, which measurements moved, and what remains uncertain. A change record prevents a polished repository from hiding the experiments that made the result possible.

If you receive feedback that a claim is too broad, narrow the claim before adding another feature. If feedback reveals an unclear setup, fix the README and test it with a fresh environment. Portfolio quality often improves through removal: fewer screenshots, fewer unsupported adjectives, fewer unrelated tools, and a clearer path to the evidence.

Use a short README at the repository root to explain the collection. Each project should have its own README with commands and evidence. Do not make the reviewer run a large application before understanding the result.

Show decisions, not just technologies

A list of tools is not a portfolio narrative. "Python, PyTorch, embeddings, Docker, Kubernetes" says little about your judgment.

A decision sentence is stronger:

> I used a time-aware split because requests from the same process changed over the year; a random split produced an estimate that did not match the intended future use.

Or:

> I kept a retrieval-only baseline because the model-generated answer could sound correct even when the required source was not retrieved.

Or:

> I did not add Kubernetes because the service had no scheduling or scaling constraint that justified the operational cost.

These statements reveal engineering thinking even when the implementation is small.

Make the evidence easy to inspect

Use a predictable repository layout. Put setup instructions near the top. State the expected time and resource requirements. Provide a small fixture or sample output when the original data cannot be shared.

Include:

- a quick-start command;
- a longer reproducibility path;
- expected output shape and approximate metrics;
- a troubleshooting section;
- a license and data-permission note;

- a contact or issue route if the repository is public.

Do not require a reader to install a GPU, create a cloud account, or provide an unknown secret merely to understand the project. If an external dependency is necessary, explain it and provide a local demonstration path where possible.

Screenshots are evidence, not the artifact

A screenshot can show a dashboard or result, but it is easy to stage and hard to inspect. Pair screenshots with code, configuration, logs, evaluation data, and a written interpretation.

For a model project, show the split, baseline, metric definitions, error analysis, and artifact contract. For an application project, show retrieval cases, unsupported behavior, citation validation, authorization tests, latency, and cost observations. For a production project, show container build, health behavior, release records, failure drills, and rollback.

A polished visual is useful when it answers a question. It should not replace the question.

Create a project index

At the root, create a one-page index:

Project 1 — data to model: the decision, model evidence, and largest failure.

Project 2 — modern AI application: the user task, retrieval boundary, evaluation, and security behavior.

Project 3 — production constraints: the service lifecycle, observability, failure drill, and rollback.

For each, include the role the project demonstrates and the role it does not demonstrate. A model project is not evidence of operating a distributed service. A container project is not evidence of advanced ML research.

Clean the repository before sharing

Search for secrets, private names, local paths, credentials, and accidental datasets. Review the Git diff and history. Remove generated caches and outputs that obscure the project. Run the setup from a clean environment.

Use tests that fail clearly. Remove dead experiments or place them in an archive with an explanation. A reviewer does not need every abandoned idea, but they benefit from seeing one or two meaningful alternatives and the reason you rejected them.

Do not rewrite history casually after sharing a repository. If sensitive data is exposed, rotate or revoke the credential first, then follow a documented cleanup process and notify affected collaborators.

Write limitations with precision

A limitation is not an apology. It tells the reader where the evidence stops.

Good limitations include:

- the data fixture is synthetic;
- the evaluation set is small;
- the corpus contains only approved documents in one language;
- human review judged a sample of answers;
- latency was measured locally;
- the cloud deployment was short-lived;
- cost estimates exclude a negotiated provider discount;
- the service has no high-availability design;
- the model was not tested in a regulated setting.

Avoid “more data and a larger model would improve it” as a generic ending. Name the uncertainty and the experiment that could reduce it.

Adapt the portfolio by path

Path A readers should lead with the experiment card, model workflow, comparison to a baseline, error analysis, reproducibility, and saved inference contract.

Path B readers should lead with the application contract, source and authorization boundary, retrieval evaluation, structured outputs, abstention, and cost/latency tradeoff.

Path C readers should lead with the service boundary, container and configuration strategy, observability, release record, failure drill, and rollback.

Keep all three projects visible. A reader can lead with one path without pretending the other engineering perspectives do not matter.

Reader artifact

Portfolio headline: ________

Primary project and role signal: ________

Project links and quick-start commands: ______

Evidence a reviewer sees in five minutes: _____

Most important failure and learning: _____

Data and privacy statement: ________

What I deliberately do not claim: ________

Next experiment: ______

Next step

Chapter 17 translates the same evidence into a resume. A resume should not introduce claims that the repositories cannot support.

CHECKLIST

Chapter checklist

- [ ] Each project explains problem, constraints, approach, evaluation, failure, reproducibility, limits, and next experiment.
- [ ] A reviewer can understand the project before running it.
- [ ] Screenshots are paired with inspectable evidence.
- [ ] The repository contains no secret or unauthorized data.
- [ ] My primary path is visible without erasing the other projects.
- [ ] I avoid calling project work professional experience.

CHAPTER 17

Translate Skills Into a Resume

A resume is a constrained interface between your evidence and a hiring decision. It is not a complete autobiography and not a keyword container. Its job is to make a credible next conversation possible.

Start with the target role

Choose one target role for each version of the resume. A Path A version may emphasize model development and evaluation. A Path B version may emphasize model-enabled applications and cloud delivery. A Path C version may emphasize deployment, reliability, and operations.

Do not write one headline that promises mastery of every path. Shared foundations can appear, but the order should match the role.

Write:

Target role: ____________

Three responsibilities it likely includes: ______

Three artifacts that prove related work: ________

One responsibility I am not yet claiming: _______

Use current job descriptions as signals, not as a specification you must copy. Employer terminology varies.

Choose the first page deliberately

The top third of the resume should answer who you are trying to become useful to and what evidence supports that direction. A short summary can state the path and strongest artifact. It should not promise a job outcome or claim seniority by aspiration.

If you are changing fields, make transferable work visible. A software developer can point to interfaces, testing, and delivery. An analyst can point to measurement, uncertainty, and decision communication. An operations practitioner can point to systems, incidents, and repeatability. Then connect those strengths to the AI engineering project rather than hiding them behind a list of tools.

Maintain a master evidence file with the longer description, repository link, dates, measured conditions, and limitations. Each role-specific resume can be shorter without losing accuracy. When a claim changes, update the evidence file and the relevant resume versions together.

Use evidence-first bullets

A strong project bullet usually contains:

- an action;
- the artifact or system;
- the method or constraint;
- an evaluation or result;
- a limitation when the result could be misunderstood.

For example:

> Built a reproducible triage-model experiment using a time-aware split and a rule baseline; compared precision/recall at a documented review threshold, inspected errors from incomplete intake fields, and published a README with setup and limitations.

This is stronger than:

> Created an AI model that improved support efficiency.

The second sentence hides the dataset, metric, comparison, and evidence. It also implies a business outcome that may not have been measured.

Quantify responsibly

Numbers can clarify scale, latency, coverage, or improvement. They can also create false authority.

State what was measured, on what data, under which conditions, and whether the number is a local experiment or a deployed outcome. “Reduced median local latency from 1.8 seconds to 1.2 seconds on a fixed fixture” is inspectable. “10x faster” without a baseline and environment is not.

Do not convert a small project metric into a company outcome. Do not claim cost savings unless cost was actually measured and the decision context is clear. Do not claim production reliability from a short local run.

Cover-letter and profile language

Use a cover letter or profile summary to connect one project to one responsibility in the target role. State the problem, the evidence, and the question you want to explore next. Avoid repeating every tool from the resume.

For example, a Path B reader might explain that a documentation assistant project made retrieval quality, authorization, and citation validation visible, and that they want to deepen those skills in a cloud application team. A Path C reader might explain how a containerized service and failure drill exposed the difference between a running process and an observable service. These are specific, defensible signals.

Do not use a profile to imply employment, production scale, or certification status that the evidence does not support. Clear scope increases trust.

Organize skills by evidence

Group skills into categories that match artifacts:

Model development: Python, tensor workflows, supervised learning, evaluation, error analysis, PyTorch.

AI application engineering: APIs, retrieval, structured output, authorization boundaries, evaluation, latency and cost measurement.

Production engineering: Linux, containers, configuration, logs, metrics, deployment, rollback, versioning.

Collaboration: Git, README documentation, tests, issue notes, design decisions.

Remove a technology from the prominent list if you cannot explain how you used it. A small honest list is more valuable than a catalog copied from a job description.

Education and credentials

List a selected credential only with its exact current name and status after verifying the official source. A planned certification is not a certification. A course completion is not the same as an externally assessed credential.

If a provider name or course is volatile, use a broader description in a durable resume version and maintain current details elsewhere. Never imply a sponsorship, partnership, or endorsement.

Tailor without fabricating

A tailored resume changes emphasis and language; it does not invent experience. Move the most relevant project up. Explain the constraint that resembles the target work. Use the employer's terminology when it is accurate.

If a posting asks for Kubernetes and your evidence is one local container, state container and production foundations rather than claiming Kubernetes operations. If a posting asks for cloud deployment and your project is local, say that you designed the cloud requirements or completed a bounded deployment experiment, not that you operated a cloud platform at scale.

A gap can be addressed with a project plan, a learning milestone, or a direct statement of scope. Misrepresentation creates a harder interview problem later.

Resume review checklist

Ask another person—or a future version of yourself—to answer:

- What role is this resume targeting?
- Which two artifacts prove the claim?
- What did the candidate personally decide?
- Which numbers are measured?
- Which claims are limited?
- What would I ask about in an interview?
- Is any technology listed without evidence?
- Could a project link be opened without a setup mystery?

If the reviewer cannot answer these questions, shorten the tool list and strengthen the evidence descriptions.

Reader artifact

Target role version: ____________

Headline claim: ________

Three evidence bullets: ____________

Measured results with conditions: __________

Primary path: _________

Deliberate scope boundary: _________

Project links: _________

Next step

Chapter 18 turns these claims into interview conversations. The objective is not to perform confidence. It is to explain decisions, evidence, failure, and learning.

CHECKLIST

Chapter checklist

- [ ] Each resume version targets one role.
- [ ] Project bullets state actions, constraints, and evidence.
- [ ] Numbers include context and do not imply unmeasured business outcomes.
- [ ] Planned credentials are labeled as planned.
- [ ] Every prominent skill appears in an artifact I can explain.
- [ ] I have not inflated project work into employment experience.

CHAPTER 18

Prepare for AI Engineering Interviews

An interview is a constrained investigation of how you think and communicate. You cannot control every question, but you can prepare a truthful path from problem to decision to evidence.

Build a story for each project

Use a six-part story:

1. What problem or user need did you choose?
2. What constraints shaped the design?
3. What did you build?
4. How did you evaluate it?
5. What failed or remained uncertain?
6. What would you do next?

Practice a two-minute version and a ten-minute version. The short version should contain enough detail to invite a useful follow-up. The long version should not become a lecture.

Do not memorize a success story without a failure. Interviewers learn more from how you diagnosed a weak result, changed one variable, or decided not to add complexity.

A four-session practice loop

In the first session, explain each project aloud without notes and record where you become vague. In the second, answer one technical question per project and draw the data or service boundary. In the third, run a failure drill and narrate what you inspect first, second, and third. In the fourth, ask another person to interrupt with a constraint change and practice revising the design without abandoning the evidence.

Review the recording for claims you cannot support, jargon that hides a decision, and answers that describe a tool before a problem. Replace those sentences with a constraint and a test. The goal is not to sound polished; it is to make your reasoning inspectable under time pressure.

Prepare one sentence for a genuine gap:

> I have not operated that at production scale. In this project I operated a bounded local service, measured the failure path, and would next test the scaling constraint by doing ______.

This statement is more useful than implying an experience you do not have.

Build a question bank from your own artifacts

Generate questions from the repository rather than memorizing generic interview lists. For each project, ask why the baseline was chosen, what would invalidate the evaluation, which dependency is most fragile, how authorization is enforced, how cost is bounded, and what you would remove if the deadline shortened.

Write one strong answer and one honest uncertainty for each question. Practice drawing the relevant boundary while speaking. If the interviewer changes the constraint—smaller budget, stricter retention, higher latency, more frequent releases—identify which decision changes first and which evidence you would collect.

This practice also exposes gaps before an interview. Return to the project and add a test or limitation rather than inventing a polished answer.

Path A questions

A Path A discussion may examine data splits, baselines, metrics, overfitting, leakage, tensor shapes, loss, gradients, optimization, evaluation modes, saved artifacts, and error analysis.

Prepare to explain why a random split could mislead, how a threshold affects precision and recall, what a batch shape means, why gradients are cleared, and how you know a saved model can be used consistently.

If you do not know an answer, state the boundary and describe how you would test it. A precise "I have not measured that; I would inspect the input contract and run a controlled comparison" is better than a confident invention.

Path B questions

A Path B discussion may examine retrieval, grounding, citations, structured outputs, prompt injection, authentication versus authorization, model failure, latency, cost, and cloud tradeoffs.

Prepare to distinguish retrieval quality from answer quality. Explain why a fluent response can be unsupported, why retrieved text is data rather than authority, and what the application does when evidence is missing.

Be ready to compare one cloud choice against requirements rather than list services. Explain what is provider-specific, what is portable, and what you would measure before scaling.

Path C questions

A Path C discussion may examine Linux processes, containers, configuration, health and readiness, logs, metrics, deployment, rollback, failure recovery, resource limits, identity, and orchestration tradeoffs.

Prepare to explain how you detect a failed release, what a rollback requires, why a service can be alive but not ready, where secrets enter, and why Kubernetes is or is not justified for the service.

Do not present a copied cluster diagram as operational experience. Explain the exact environment you ran and the limitations of the exercise.

Whiteboard the failure path

A useful practice prompt is:

> The service returns a plausible answer with the wrong citation. What do you inspect first?

Possible reasoning:

- check whether the correct source was retrieved;
- inspect chunk and metadata boundaries;
- verify citation validation;
- compare the structured result with the displayed result;
- run a test case that isolates retrieval from generation;
- decide whether the fix belongs in the corpus, retriever, parser, or policy layer.

Another prompt:

> Validation performance fell after a new data release.

Reasoning:

- verify the split and target definition;
- compare distributions and missingness;
- check preprocessing fit and feature order;
- inspect duplicate or time-shifted records;
- reproduce the previous release;
- revert if the new result violates the acceptance condition.

The value is the sequence of investigation, not the most impressive vocabulary.

Explain tradeoffs

Every technology choice should have a reason and a cost.

A managed service may reduce operations effort but increase provider dependence or cost. A larger model may improve answer quality but increase latency and expense. More retrieval context may improve coverage but dilute relevance and raise token use. A cache may reduce repeated cost but create staleness. A stricter refusal policy may reduce harmful unsupported answers but increase escalations.

Practice stating both sides. “I chose X because A; I accepted B; I would revisit it if C changed” is an engineering answer.

Ask better questions

At the end of an interview, ask about:

- the decisions the role owns;
- how model or application quality is evaluated;
- the boundary between research, application, and production teams;
- deployment and rollback practices;
- incident learning;
- how cloud and vendor choices are made;
- what evidence would define success in the first months.

Avoid questions that imply you already understand a system you have not seen. Curiosity is more credible when it is specific.

Interview evidence card

For each project, prepare:

One-sentence problem: ________

Most important constraint: __________

Measured evaluation: __________

Failure I investigated: _______

Decision I changed: ___________

Current limitation: ___________

Next experiment: ________

Next step

Chapter 19 turns the roadmap into a twelve-month sequence. It includes a first month for evidence, a middle period for depth, and later decisions about specialization without requiring you to predict an entire career today.

CHECKLIST

Chapter checklist

- [ ] I can explain each project in two minutes and ten minutes.
- [ ] I can name a failure and the investigation sequence.
- [ ] I can distinguish measured results from assumptions.
- [ ] I can explain one tradeoff for each major tool.
- [ ] I have a truthful answer for every prominent resume skill.
- [ ] I prepared questions about ownership, evaluation, deployment, and learning.

CHAPTER 19

Your Next 12 Months

A twelve-month roadmap is a sequence of review points, not a prediction of a job title. Your target role, available time, health, finances, and the market can change. The purpose is to make the next decision easier while preserving evidence from the previous one.

Months 1–2: establish the working direction

Complete the role and path decision from Chapter 3. Finish the foundation assessment. Choose one project domain and write the first contract.

Your outputs should include:

- a selected primary path and a "not now" list;
- a clean Python repository;
- a small experiment card;
- a first weekly schedule;
- a documented gap that will be repaired.

Do not add three cloud subscriptions or several certificates during this period. The question is whether the selected work is interesting and feasible enough to pursue.

Months 3–4: complete the first evidence cycle

Finish Project 1 through baseline, model, evaluation, and failure analysis. If Path A is primary, implement the PyTorch extension. If Path B or C is primary, still complete the model evidence so that later application or production decisions have a foundation.

At the end of this period, ask:

- Can I explain the data and target?
- Can another person reproduce the result?
- What failed?
- Which gap should the next project address?
- Did the path become more or less attractive after doing the work?

A change of path at this point is a useful discovery, not wasted work.

Months 5–6: build the application layer

Complete Project 2. Build the corpus manifest, retrieval baseline, structured output, citations, abstention, evaluation cases, and security boundary. If Path B is primary, perform the cloud comparison and Chapter 12 decision here.

If Path A is primary, use Project 2 to learn how model artifacts become application behavior. If Path C is primary, use it to identify the operational boundaries that Project 3 will need.

Choose a credential only if the relevant gate produced Decision A. A deliberate later or none decision remains valid.

Months 7–8: operate the system

Complete Project 3. Containerize the service, separate configuration and secrets, add health and readiness behavior, define observability, run a failure drill, and record a release and rollback.

If Path C is primary, perform the Chapter 13 milestone decision. If Path A or B is primary, use the production work to understand the deployment and lifecycle skills your target role requires.

Do not confuse a cloud console screenshot with operating evidence. Document what was measured, what was local, what was temporary, and what remains untested.

Months 9–10: consolidate career evidence

Create the portfolio index, targeted resume version, project stories, and interview cards. Ask for review from someone who can challenge unclear claims.

Remove or rewrite claims that cannot be supported. Improve one project README and one failure analysis. A smaller portfolio with clear boundaries is more credible than a large collection of disconnected demos.

If a selected credential is still useful, use the current official page to verify status and policies. Schedule only when the readiness card supports it.

Months 11–12: choose the next depth

Review the year as an evidence set:

- which work did you enjoy owning;
- which failures did you keep investigating;
- which artifact improved most;
- which responsibility remains uncomfortable;
- which target roles still appear relevant;
- which credential or learning route solves a current gap;
- which path should remain secondary.

Choose one next depth:

- Path A: stronger model evaluation, serving, optimization, or domain depth;
- Path B: deeper cloud architecture, application reliability, retrieval evaluation, or security;
- Path C: deeper Linux, platform operations, orchestration, reliability, or cost control;
- a new role hypothesis based on evidence.

Do not turn the next depth into a shopping list. Name one project, one measurable capability, and one review date.

Maintain a living decision record

Keep a short record with:

Current path: ________

Current role hypothesis: ___________

Strongest evidence: ________

Most important gap: ________

Next project or milestone: _______

Review date: ________

Reason the path could change: _____

Update it after each major project or work change. The record prevents the roadmap from becoming a document you read once and forget.

If the path changes

The first path is a working hypothesis. A Path A reader may discover that model debugging is less appealing than application design. A Path B reader may enjoy the document and evaluation boundary but not cloud operations. A Path C reader may discover that reliability and deployment work is the part they want to own.

When the path changes, preserve the shared foundation and reuse the project evidence. Reframe Project 1 as model literacy, Project 2 as application evidence, or Project 3 as operational evidence. Write what changed your mind. A documented change is stronger than pretending the original plan was always correct.

The path can also change because the target role changes. A smaller organization may combine application and production work. A larger organization may separate them. Use responsibilities and artifacts as the stable reference, not a title that one employer uses differently.

Review the roadmap like a system

At the end of the year, inspect not only outputs but the process that produced them. Which tasks generated useful evidence? Which tasks consumed time without changing a decision? Where did documentation prevent a repeated mistake? Which external information became stale?

Update the roadmap itself. Remove a resource that no longer exists, clarify a term that caused confusion, and keep a dated note for a volatile change. A living roadmap is maintained like software: with ownership, review, and a reason for each change.

Monthly review template

At the end of each month, save one page with four headings: evidence created, evidence challenged, decision changed, and next experiment. Link the repository commit, evaluation run, deployment record, or conversation that supports each entry.

If the page contains only hours studied, convert the next month's goal into an artifact. If it contains only output, add a review or failure test. If it contains only failures, choose one smaller experiment that can produce a clean comparison. This rhythm keeps the roadmap balanced between action, reflection, and recovery.

When progress is slower

A slower year can still produce strong evidence. Reduce scope before reducing honesty. Build a smaller dataset, a narrower corpus, a local service, or one failure drill. Keep the same decision and evidence structure.

If work or life interrupts the plan, preserve the repository and write a restart note: where you stopped, what worked, what failed, and the first command to run. A restartable project is an engineering artifact.

Do not borrow money, claim experience you do not have, or schedule a credential under pressure merely to preserve an imagined timeline. The roadmap is meant to support a sustainable decision.

Reader artifact

Twelve-month outcome I can defend: ________

Primary path: ________

Project evidence I will publish: __________

One credential decision, if any: __________

Review dates: __________

Scope I deliberately exclude: ______

Person who will review my claims: __________

Next step

Use the conclusion to choose that first action. Then close the book and do it while the decision is still concrete.

CHECKLIST

Chapter checklist

- [ ] I turned the year into review points rather than a single promise.
- [ ] Every period produces an artifact or decision.
- [ ] I can change path without discarding the evidence already built.
- [ ] My credential choices follow a real need.
- [ ] I recorded scope boundaries and review dates.
- [ ] I know the first fifteen-minute action after finishing this book.

CONCLUSION

You Now Have a Path

You do not need to know every tool in AI to take a useful next step. You need a role hypothesis, an evidence-based starting point, a path, a project, and a way to review what happened.

Path A emphasizes model development, evaluation, PyTorch, and the discipline of making an experiment reproducible. Path B emphasizes model-enabled applications, retrieval, evaluation, authorization, cloud choice, and deliberate use of current credentials. Path C emphasizes Linux, containers, deployment, observability, lifecycle, and production milestones that match real responsibility.

The paths share foundations and eventually meet in production reality. They are not three identities you must collect at once.

The QR resources are optional and current by design. They may help you save an assessment, use a project template, check a volatile policy, or compare a selected credential. They are not the book's value. If every affiliate program disappears, the decision gates, projects, evidence records, and first-party sources remain.

Choose one action that fits fifteen minutes:

- write the first project contract;
- create the repository;
- run the baseline;
- inspect one PyTorch batch;
- define the application corpus;
- build the container;
- schedule the first protected work block.

Write the action here:

Do it before searching for another course. A roadmap becomes real when it changes what you do next.

Sources & Further Reading

Role and career framing

Role and career framing

- U.S. Bureau of Labor Statistics, Software Developers, Quality Assurance Analysts, and Testers.
- U.S. Bureau of Labor Statistics, Data Scientists.
- O*NET OnLine, Computer and Information Research Scientists.
- Google Cloud, Professional Machine Learning Engineer role and certification materials.
- AWS, current certification catalog.
- Microsoft Learn, current credentials catalog and credential-retirement notices.

Python, data, and machine learning

- Python Documentation, Python Tutorial.
- Python Packaging User Guide, Installing Packages.
- NumPy User Guide.
- scikit-learn Getting Started.
- scikit-learn Cross-validation: evaluating estimator performance.
- scikit-learn Metrics and scoring.
- scikit-learn Common pitfalls and recommended practices.

PyTorch

- PyTorch, Learn the Basics.
- PyTorch, Quickstart.
- PyTorch, Optimizing Model Parameters.
- PyTorch, Reproducibility notes.
- PyTorch data-loading documentation.

Cloud, production, and security

- Docker documentation, What is a container?
- Kubernetes documentation, Concepts and overview.
- Git documentation.
- GitHub documentation on repositories, secret handling, and removing sensitive data.
- NIST AI Risk Management Framework and Generative AI Profile for readers who need a governance vocabulary.
- OWASP guidance for web and AI application security, used as a starting point rather than a substitute for a threat model.

Credential sources

- Linux Foundation certification catalog and individual credential pages.
- Linux Foundation education terms, exam retake, refund, and FAQ pages.
- AWS certification catalog and exam guides.
- Microsoft Learn credential catalog and retirement page.
- Google Cloud certification catalog and individual certification pages.

How to use this list

Prefer the official owner for a technical behavior, credential scope, policy, or product condition. Treat provider marketing and affiliate pages as commercial evidence only. Record the access date and check changes before publication or purchase.

Book Updates & Errata

Contents

Contents

Practical Notebook maintains a publisher-controlled updates page for changed links, corrected examples, volatile certification details, and material errata.

Readers should report:

- a broken source or QR destination;
- a code example that no longer matches the documented library behavior;
- a misleading claim or unclear limitation;
- an inaccessible project instruction;
- a credential or policy change that affects a decision gate.

An update does not silently change the reader's printed decision. It explains what changed, when it changed, and which part of the roadmap remains durable.

Use the current updates page when a printed link or provider detail matters:

https://practicalnotebook.com/ai-engineer/updates

CURRENT INFORMATION

Book Updates and Errata

Scan to check source corrections, changed provider details, link changes, and edition notes before relying on a time-sensitive detail.

Check book updates and errata

www.practicalnotebook.com/the-ai-engineer-roadmap/updates

Glossary

Contents

Contents

Abstention: a deliberate response that says the system lacks enough evidence to answer safely or usefully.

Artifact: an inspectable output such as a repository, experiment record, model state, README, evaluation report, service image, or runbook.

Baseline: a simple reference method used to judge whether a more complex approach adds value.

Batch: a group of examples processed together during model training or evaluation.

Cloud ecosystem: a provider's connected services, identity model, deployment tools, data services, and operational conventions.

Data leakage: information from evaluation or future conditions entering training or preprocessing in a way that makes performance look better than it will be.

Deployment: placing a software service or model workflow into an environment where it can be used.

Embedding: a numerical representation used to compare the semantic relationship between items such as text passages.

Evaluation set: examples reserved to measure behavior against defined expectations.

Feature: an input variable used by a model.

Foundation model: a broadly trained model that can be adapted or prompted for multiple tasks. The term does not guarantee accuracy or suitability.

Generalization: behavior on relevant unseen cases rather than only on training examples.

Gradient: a direction and magnitude describing how a change in parameters affects a loss under local conditions.

Inference: using a trained or configured model to produce an output for new input.

MLOps: practices that make machine-learning development, delivery, monitoring, and lifecycle management repeatable.

Observability: the ability to understand system behavior from outputs such as logs, metrics, and traces.

Orchestration: coordinating containers or services through scheduling, networking, health, scaling, and desired-state mechanisms.

Portfolio evidence: an inspectable artifact and explanation that demonstrates a capability; it is not automatically professional experience.

Prompt injection: an attempt to influence an AI application by placing instructions in user input or retrieved content that conflict with the application's intended rules.

Retrieval: selecting potentially relevant documents or passages for an application or model.

Rollback: returning a service, configuration, corpus, or release to a previously known state.

Structured output: a response constrained to a declared schema so that an application can validate fields and values before display or action.

Target: the outcome a supervised-learning model is trained to predict.

Threshold: a decision boundary applied to a score or probability to produce an action or class.

Validation: a development-stage check used to make choices without consuming the final held-out test estimate.

Versioned source of truth: the current authoritative record for a changing fact, such as an official credential page or a publisher-controlled update page.

Appendix — Reusable Review Sheets

Project contract sheet

Project contract sheet

Project name: __________

Primary path: A / B / C

User or operator: ____________

Problem statement: ____________

Decision or action supported: ______

What the system will not do: _______

Input unit: ____________

Prediction or request moment: ______

Available information: _______

Privacy and access boundary: _______

Time, cost, and reliability constraint: _________

Human review or override: __________

Success condition: ____________

Failure condition: ____________

Removal or pause condition: ________

Next fifteen-minute action: _________

Experiment record

Run identifier: _______

Hypothesis: ____________

Data or corpus version: ______

Split or evaluation version: _______

Configuration reference: ____________

Baseline: ______________

Change made: ____________

Expected effect: _______

Observed result: _______

Metric conditions: ____________

Largest changed error group: _______

Reproducibility command: ____________

Decision: keep / revert / investigate

Next experiment: _______

A good experiment record can be read by someone who was not present when the run happened. If a result cannot be reproduced, record the uncertainty rather than silently replacing it.

Retrieval evaluation sheet

Use this for Project 2. The goal is to separate the retrieval question from the answer question.

Case identifier: _______

Question category: answerable / multi-source / ambiguous / unsupported / conflicting / restricted / injection attempt

Authorized corpus scope: ____________

Required source or section: ________

Retrieved source identifiers: _______

Required evidence retrieved: yes / partial / no

Irrelevant or conflicting passages: _______

Answer supported by retrieved evidence: yes / partial / no

Citation points to the evidence: yes / no

Abstention or escalation appropriate: yes / no

User-visible result: __________

Failure class: retrieval / generation / citation / authorization / policy / latency / cost

Next test: ____________

Do not mark a response correct merely because it sounds useful. Ask whether the user could verify the answer from the permitted source.

Service release sheet

Use this for Project 3.

Release identifier: __________

Source revision: _______

Container image identifier: ________

Dependency and runtime versions: _________

Corpus or index version: __________

Model or provider identifier: ______

Configuration reference: __________

Health check result: ________

Readiness check result: ______

Evaluation result: __________

Latency and cost observations: _____

Known limitation: ___________

Rollback target: _______

Operator who reviewed: _______

Date: __________

A release is not complete until the rollback target and limitations are written. If there is no known rollback target, the release is a risk decision that should be explicit.

Failure drill sheet

Failure scenario: ____________

How the failure is detected: _______

User-visible behavior: _______

Immediate safe action: _______

Information to inspect: _______

Retry or no-retry decision: ________

Fallback: _____________

Rollback or repair: __________

Validation before reopening: _______

Owner and escalation path: ________

Learning to record: __________

Run the drill with a fixture or controlled dependency failure. Do not create a real outage merely to make a portfolio screenshot.

Evidence review for a peer

Give this sheet to a reviewer who did not build the project.

In five minutes, I understood: _____

The first unclear term was: ________

The strongest evidence was: ________

The most important unsupported claim was: _______

The setup command worked: yes / no / partly

The failure analysis was: clear / partial / missing

The limitation that matters most is: ______

One question I would ask in an interview: ________

One change that would make the README easier to trust: _______

The author response:

Change accepted: _______

Reason if not accepted: ______

Next review date: ____________

Peer review is not an endorsement. It is a test of whether another person can understand and challenge the evidence.

Certification decision sheet

Selected path: A / B / C

Credential category: _________

Official owner and page: ___________

Access date: __________

Current status verified: ______

What the scope may signal: ________

What it does not prove: ______

Project evidence already complete: ________

Project evidence still missing: _____

Current policy links checked: _______

Registration decision: _______

Scheduling decision: _________

Reason to postpone or decline: ______

Next review date: ____________

Never fill the official name or code from memory when the exact current status affects a purchase. Link the current page and record the access date.

Source update sheet

Use this when a link, library, credential, or provider changes.

Source identifier: __________

Old fact or link: ______

Observed change date: _______

New official source: ________

What remains durable: _______

Print text affected: _________

QR destination affected: __________

Claims ledger update: _______

Volatile register update: __________

Reviewer: ____________

Publication decision: update online / revise manuscript / hold publication

A change record should explain the decision, not merely replace a URL. Readers need to know whether the change affects their next action.

Monthly roadmap review

Evidence created this month: ______

Evidence challenged: ________

Decision that changed: ______

Failure that taught me something: ________

Resource or provider that became stale: ________

Next experiment: ______

Capacity adjustment: ________

One thing I will remove: __________

Next review date: ____________

A monthly review prevents the roadmap from becoming a static promise. It also creates a trace of how your role hypothesis changed.

Final publication self-audit

Before sharing a project or manuscript excerpt, check:

- [ ] The problem is understandable without the tool list.
- [ ] The evidence is reproducible or the limitation is clear.
- [ ] The metric has a definition and conditions.
- [ ] Failures and uncertainty are visible.
- [ ] Private data and secrets are absent.
- [ ] Current claims have an official source and access date.
- [ ] Volatile information is routed to the update page.
- [ ] Affiliate relationships are disclosed and optional.
- [ ] No credential, employer, or income guarantee is implied.
- [ ] The artifact remains useful if every provider link disappears.

Appendix — Practice Lab Variants

Variant A — Forecast a bounded operational quantity

Variant A — Forecast a bounded operational quantity

Choose a numeric outcome that is observable and not high-stakes: next-day inventory requests for a fictional warehouse, expected processing time for a batch, or the number of routine support requests in a time window.

Define the time at which the forecast is made. Remove features that would be known only after the period ends. Compare a constant or seasonal baseline with one model. Use a time-aware split. Report error in the target's units and show where the forecast is systematically weak.

The important evidence is not the algorithm. It is the decision about what "next day" means, how missing periods are treated, and which uncertainty the forecast leaves unresolved.

Variant B — Inspect a text-classification boundary

Create a small, permitted collection of synthetic messages with categories such as billing question, technical question, access question, and out of scope. Define a refusal category. Keep the label guide next to the data.

Start with a lexical baseline. Inspect messages with ambiguous wording and categories that overlap. Report how often the classifier asks for clarification or routes to a human. Do not claim that a text model understands intent in a general sense; show the narrow label contract.

This variant connects to Path B because it makes input validation, category drift, and human escalation visible before adding a model-generated answer.

Variant C — Detect a synthetic telemetry anomaly

Generate or use permitted numerical telemetry for a small fictional service: request latency, error count, queue depth, or memory usage. Define what an anomaly means operationally and which false alarms are acceptable.

Compare a simple threshold or rolling statistic with one anomaly method. Split by time. Show how a deployment or traffic change affects the signal. Add a runbook entry for what the operator does after an alert.

This variant connects to Path C because the output is not a diagnosis. It is a signal that must be interpreted alongside logs, deployment history, and system context.

Variant D — Reproduce a result under a changed constraint

Take one completed project and change one constraint: half the available memory, a smaller request budget, a new document version, a stricter retention rule, or a slower dependency.

Record what breaks first. Then choose one adaptation and measure its cost. You may reduce model size, change retrieval count, add a timeout, simplify the corpus, or change the evaluation target. Explain what quality was preserved and what quality was traded away.

This is a strong interview exercise because it demonstrates that engineering is not only building under ideal assumptions.

Variant E — Compare one provider adapter

Keep the core application contract unchanged and replace one adapter: local retrieval with managed search, a local model with a hosted endpoint, or a local container with a managed deployment. Do not build two complete products.

Measure the boundary you care about: setup time, latency, cost, authorization, portability, or observability. Record what became easier and what became provider-specific. Delete the experiment's temporary resources and write the cleanup steps.

The result is not a claim that one provider is universally best. It is evidence that you can make a bounded comparison.

Variant review questions

For any variant, ask:

- What is the unit of data or request?
- What information exists at the decision moment?
- What is the simplest useful baseline?
- What failure would matter most?
- Which split or evaluation set answers the real question?
- What is the smallest artifact another person can inspect?
- What would make you stop using the result?
- What did the constraint change reveal?

If you cannot answer these questions, the variant is not ready for a portfolio. Return to the core project contract.

Appendix — Interview Question Bank

Shared questions

Shared questions

- What user decision did your project support?
- Which assumption was most likely to be wrong?
- What did you measure, and under what conditions?
- What was your baseline?
- What failed?
- How did you decide what to change next?
- What would you remove if the deadline were half as long?
- Which part of the result is not transferable to a different environment?
- What would make you stop using the system?
- Which artifact would you show first to a reviewer?

Path A questions

- Why was your split appropriate for the prediction moment?
- What leakage risk did you investigate?
- What does one batch look like at the model boundary?
- Why does the chosen loss match the output and target contract?
- What changed when you modified the model?
- How did you select a threshold?
- What does the saved artifact require at inference time?
- Which error group mattered more than the average metric?
- What would you test before making the model available to users?
- What would a PyTorch credential add beyond your project evidence?

Path B questions

- How do you know the required source was retrieved?
- What happens when sources conflict?
- Why is the model allowed to synthesize but not to take an external action?
- How do you validate citations?
- How do authentication and authorization differ in your service?
- What is your behavior when the model provider times out?
- How do you bound cost?
- What did your cloud comparison measure?
- Which part of your design is portable and which is provider-specific?
- What would change before selecting a cloud credential?

Path C questions

- What is the difference between a process being alive and a service being ready?
- Where do configuration and secrets enter the container?
- How do you detect a failed release?
- What is your rollback target?
- Which logs are useful and which data should not be logged?
- Why did you or did you not use Kubernetes?
- What operational problem would justify orchestration?
- How do you compare a local run with a managed deployment?
- Which failure drill did you rehearse?
- What would a production milestone add beyond the service artifact?

Questions to ask an employer

- Which decisions does this role own directly?
- How is model or application quality evaluated?
- What is the boundary between research, application, and production work?
- How are deployment and rollback handled?
- Which failures have changed the team's practices?
- How are cloud and vendor choices made?
- What would a useful first project look like?
- Which evidence would show progress in the first three months?
- How does the team handle uncertainty or unsupported model output?
- What part of the role is intentionally not owned by this team?

Write the answer to one question you cannot currently answer. Turn that gap into a project test or a question for the next conversation.

> **End of Phase 3 manuscript drafting.** Final editorial audit and artifact generation remain.

www.ingramcontent.com/pod-product-compliance
Lightning Source LLC
LaVergne TN
LVHW010720061126
851857LV00014B/1283
* 9 7 8 2 4 8 9 4 8 3 9 9 4 *